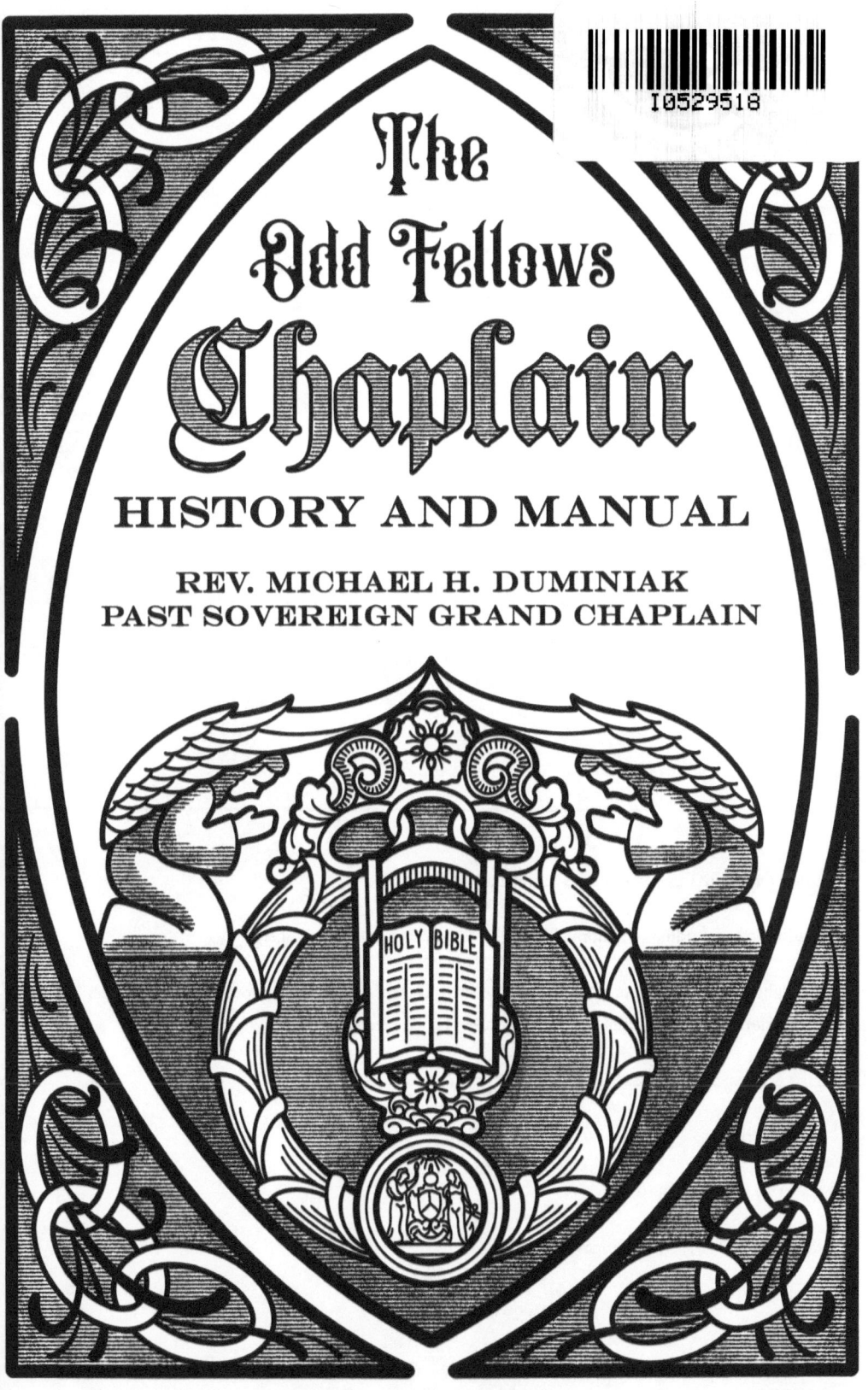

# The Odd Fellows Chaplain

## HISTORY AND MANUAL

### REV. MICHAEL H. DUMINIAK
### PAST SOVEREIGN GRAND CHAPLAIN

HOLY BIBLE

# Preface

It has been a great honor to serve as Sovereign Grand Chaplain of the Independent Order of Odd Fellows. I have considered it a deeply important responsibility and given it my best effort.

Serving as a Chaplain in our Order is an important function regardless of the level at which you serve. The Sovereign Grand Chaplain has a much broader latitude in the performance of the office than a lodge Chaplain does, but a lodge Chaplain has more regular influence for the benefit of the Order.

The Sovereign Grand Chaplain opens the daily sessions of the Sovereign Grand Lodge with a lesson and a prayer that are not provided as a standardized ritual. Similarly, the Sovereign Grand Chaplain has a role in almost every function throughout the year without any specified language. It can be a daunting challenge to simultaneously provide a message that is spiritually moving and also universally acceptable.

The ambiguity surrounding the Chaplain's role is an area that I felt needed some clarification. I believe that every Odd Fellow who accepts any office within the Order does so with a desire to do the best job possible. The lack of clarity for the duties of a lodge Chaplain is a problem for which I strove to find a solution.

Additionally, there has been a small amount of denigration of the office of Chaplain in recent years. Some have called for its removal based on claims that it is a relatively modern innovation, antithetical to original Odd Fellowship. Not only are these claims demonstrably false, but even if they were true, the role of the Chaplain is far more than just someone who reads prayers from the ritual. It seemed to me that, at least for those members and perhaps for many more, there was a lack of understanding about the role the Chaplain has played and continues to play in our Order.

Finally, I felt it was incumbent upon me as the Sovereign Grand Chaplain to do something to address these issues. I am not one to just say that something should be done; I am one who sees a need and then takes action to address it. This Manual is not an official product of the Independent Order of Odd Fellows, but rather my best effort to explain the materials provided to Chaplains by the Order.

This book is my attempt to help correct misconceptions, aid understanding, and provide clarity for any person who holds the office of Chaplain. Knowing the challenge I have faced in writing universally acceptable prayers for use at various events for which the ritual provides no standard prayer, I have also included a section of prayers a Chaplain could use at banquets and other gatherings.

I am an Odd Fellow. I am also a Christian and an ordained minister. In my own faith, I follow an Anglo-Catholic tradition within the Episcopal Church. For those unfamiliar with that tradition, it involves a lot of ceremony with specified vestments to wear, ceremonial actions to perform (such as the use of incense, bells, and movements), and a prayer book of standardized prayers that often end with the Sign of the Cross and invocation of the Trinity.

I know that if I were to offer prayers at an Odd Fellows banquet in the same form as my faith tradition, I would alienate the majority of those in attendance who do not have a faith tradition of performing the Sign of the Cross while invoking the Trinity, let alone being enveloped in a cloud of incense. I believe it is that self-awareness that my faith tradition is not universal that has allowed me to better understand the broader nature of belief we share as Odd Fellows and the importance of respecting everyone's personal faith tradition by not pushing one's own.

Therefore, I offer to you, my Brothers and Sisters in Odd Fellowship, this Chaplain History and Manual to help you understand the duties of the office, its history, its importance, and to provide helpful guidance and resources for you to fulfill it in a manner that includes all members, regardless of their faith tradition.

Rev. M.H. Duminiak

# ACKNOWLEDGEMENTS

The following individuals contributed their thoughts on the topic of Chaplains and prayer within the lodge, helping to provide additional insight into the role:

Linnea Bredenberg

Andrew Daggett

Jesse Donaldson

Michael Greenzeiger

Toby Hanson

Ainslie Heilich

Howard Malin

Tom McDonald

Elizabeth Mowry-Harbstreit

William Sanderson

Tyson Seiger

# DEDICATION

I dedicate this book to two individuals who provided the most significant influence on me towards its creation.

To the late Past Sovereign Grand Master Charles "Buddy" Worrell, a friend and mentor in the Order who was also an ordained and practicing minister. He served as an excellent example of how to live the values of his faith within Odd Fellowship, bringing compassion, understanding, and conciliation while leaving behind all the faith-tradition-specific phrases. He also supported me in seeking ordination when I expressed a felt calling.

To Gerald V. "Jerry" Workman, the Sovereign Grand Master who appointed me to be the Sovereign Grand Chaplain during his term, a friend and a mentor in the Order. His strong commitment to his own faith tradition shines through in all his actions and guides him to find the solution to a problem that not only complies with the rules and tenets of our Order, but also brings compassion and harmony as balm to ease the tensions and hurt that accompany any problem. He rules by the lesson of the Sword & Scales, reasons by the lessons of the Holy Bible, and lives by the lesson of the Heart in Hand.

# INTRODUCTION

Welcome to being a Chaplain! If you're reading this book, you are probably wondering about the full scope of your duties because you have already looked through the ritual and the Code of General Laws and come up almost empty. That is why this guide was written.

It is an oddity in Odd Fellowship that the Chaplain of an Odd Fellows lodge is the only officer who has no clearly specified duties. There are necessary parts in rituals and ceremonies designated for the Chaplain, but nowhere in our ritual or Code of General Laws is there a statement of the specific duties of this office.

Even in the Rebekahs, Encampment, and Canton, the duties of a Chaplain are somewhat vague. The Code of General Laws simply states that "The Chaplain will perform such duties as pertain to the office." This description does not provide any enlightenment on the specifics of those duties.

*The Odd Fellows Chaplain History and Manual* seeks to fill that void by referencing the duties of this role as they appear across branches, and extrapolating them through an examination of historical information and various rituals and ceremonies.

For the purposes of this Manual, the use of the office "Chaplain" covers all branches and, in the special case of the High Priest of an Encampment, refers only to the non-executive functions of that office.

This manual will provide you with not only a better understanding of the role of Chaplain, but also the specific resources, information, liturgy, and ritual needed to carry it out successfully.

This book contains rituals not found in the main ritual of each branch, guidelines for performing your duties, resources for effective counseling, and a collection of standard prayers for various occasions. With this information, you can confidently understand and carry out your important duties.

# HISTORY OF THE CHAPLAIN

Odd Fellowship has always had a requirement for belief in a Supreme Being and has always had prayers at various points, but it did not always have a designated Chaplain. In the early years, the opening and closing of a lodge was a shorter affair and did not always include any standard prayers. However, modern assertions that there was no Chaplain, nor any prayers, in the opening and closing of lodges are entirely erroneous.

The Bylaws of the Grand Lodge of the United States in 1841 presented for its incorporation in the State of Maryland, approved by the Assembly on February 10, 1842,[1] includes the following Article 24: "All Grand and subordinate lodges and encampments under this jurisdiction shall at all times open and close their regular meetings with prayer."[2]

---

1. *Journal of Proceedings 1821-1843*, Grand Lodge of the United States (1844) p. xi

2. *Journal of Proceedings 1821-1843*, Grand Lodge of the United States (1844) p. xxv

This demonstrates clearly that there were not only prayers, but also that they were mandatory in Odd Fellows during its early period.

At the 1847 session of the Grand Lodge of the United States, Article 24 had been amended to read: "All Grand and Subordinate lodges and encampments under this jurisdiction may at all times open and close their meetings with prayer."[3]

This loosening of the requirement can be traced through various decisions related to the lack of a Chaplain at various times and in certain lodges. For example, in the 1853 Digest (the precursor to the Code of General Laws), the difference between "may" have a prayer and "required" to have a prayer was addressed in a decision rendered in 1852 when Trenton Lodge appealed a censure it received from the Grand Lodge of New Jersey for disobeying the Grand Master's order to open and close their meetings with a prayer.

The appeal was granted on the grounds that "proper persons are not always in attendance to offer prayer" and that lodges should have prayers when it is practical.[4]   An effort to repeal Article 24 is recorded in the same 1853 Digest: "A proposition to strike out the 24th article, requiring Grand and Subordinate Bodies to open and close their meetings with prayer, rejected."[5]

These examples illustrate that the bylaws of the Order already had provision for prayers from the time of incorporation, a majority of represen-

---

3. *Annual Communication*, Grand Lodge of the United States (1847) p. 965

4. *1853 Digest*, Grand Lodge of the United States, (1854) p. 136

5. *1853 Digest*, Grand Lodge of the United States, (1854) p. 165

tatives rejected the effort to remove that requirement, and flexibility was allowed due to particular lodge circumstances. Prayer was not a new and innovative part of Odd Fellowship injected in the early 20th century. It was an integral part of the Order from its earliest days, despite the ritual not specifying the content of the prayers or a required office of Chaplain.

While there was no uniformity across the Order, various jurisdictions had their own set of prayers. One example is the prayer adopted by the Grand Lodge of New York,[6] which utilized the role of Chaplain.[7] Others would simply designate a member to perform prayers as needed without holding an office. Invocations of God took place in the degrees, with the Bible as one of the three symbols of the Fifth Degree.[8] The requirement to have the Bible present in the lodge room was adopted in 1875.[9] The current opening and closing lodge prayers, with but slight modern alteration for gender, remain those which were prepared by Bro. Venable, Grand Chaplain, adopted in 1882.[10]

The lack of a specified Chaplain would appear to be a result of the variety of customs and procedures of the various jurisdictions during the developmental years of the Order. While the lodges were not required to

---

6. *The Odd Fellows Manual,* A. B. Grosh (1852) p. 181

7. The Odd Fellows Manual, A. B. Grosh (1852) p. 218

8. *History of American Odd Fellowship: The First Decade* by James L. Ridgely (1878) P. 503

9. *1903 Digest,* Sovereign Grand Lodge (1904) p.505

10. *1903 Digest,* Sovereign Grand Lodge (1904) p.506

have a Chaplain, Grand Lodges had Grand Chaplains and Encampments had High Priests.

Various foundational books about the operation of the Order, such as *The Odd Fellows Manual* by A. B. Grosh (1852), *The Odd-Fellow's Improved Manual* by the same author (1868), *History of American Odd Fellowship: The First Decade* by James L. Ridgely (1878), and *The Independent Order of Odd Fellows' Ritualistic, Secret, and Floor Work* by F. Walker (1887) all describe the presence of various prayers within our rituals at that time as well as the role of Chaplain, although it varied by jurisdiction.

Walker's book contains, on page 4,[11] a diagram of a lodge room in which the Chaplain's station is shown exactly where it is today, even though the opening and closing ritual provided on the following pages does not include a codified prayer nor mention of any duties for the Chaplain. It does not include any duties for the Scene Supporters either, although they are similarly shown on the diagram and did have a purpose in degree rituals. For that matter, there is no Treasurer included in the opening ritual, although the office is mentioned by the Permanent Secretary (Financial Secretary) and obviously was an essential part of the functioning of a lodge. Also, in Grosh's 1852 book, he describes not only the office of Chaplain but also the Jewel, Regalia, Station, and Duties of the office based on the standard customs.[12]

---

11. *The Independent Order of Odd Fellows' Ritualistic, Secret, and Floor Work* by F. Walker (1887) p. 4

12. *The Odd Fellows Manual,* A. B. Grosh (1852) p. 211-222

The point being made here is that assertions by some modern Odd Fellow "historians" that there was no Chaplain prior to the first quarter of the twentieth century are simply false conclusions arrived at by performing only a cursory glance at old rituals and not any true scholarship that examines recorded practices and adopted decisions.

When the eminent James Ridgely revised the ritual of the Order, he rewrote the degrees, as well as the opening and closing rituals.[13]  While the ritual of the early twentieth century did not have a specified part for the office of Chaplain, it did specify opening and closing prayers, which were either performed by a Chaplain (as shown on the lodge diagram) or another person so designated.[14]  That was left up to the custom of the jurisdiction, as it had been prior to the revisions.

A standardized ritual for all jurisdictions came into being, in 1928, which codified the Chaplain position. The Chaplain has been a listed officer of lodges continuously since that time.  That the Odd Fellows Subordinate Lodge Ritual still does not include a part for the Chaplain in the Rehearsal of Duties is a curious artifact of our heterogeneous origins.

The same cannot be said of the Encampments.  From the creation of the Encampment branch, there was always a High Priest.  It speaks to the custom and practice of early Odd Fellowship that the role of High Priest was considered essential, most likely indicating that the role of a Chaplain was already, by that time, generally considered essential in lodges.  It is also of note that the Chaplain's duties were combined with an elective line

---

13. *Odd Fellows Monitor and Guide,* T.G. Beharrell (1888) p. 35

14. *1903 Digest,* Sovereign Grand Lodge (1904) p.506

officer in Encampment. This would seem to indicate that the common practice, mentioned in the Digest,[15] of the Noble Grand offering prayers if there was no Chaplain present, influenced the development of the Encampment ritual to designate one of the elective officers to perform the duties of a Chaplain. The Encampment became the only branch in which a Chaplain is an elected officer, serving under the title of High Priest.

The Chaplain in a Rebekah lodge followed a similar path to the Odd Fellows lodge, but in a compressed timeline. The original degree, first offered in 1851,[16] was conferred by Odd Fellows lodges and used the officers of those lodges.[17]  Independent Rebekah lodges were not authorized until 1868. By that time, the role of Chaplain had long been a regular feature of Odd Fellowship. As a result, the Rebekah lodge ritual included the office of Chaplain located in the same place as in an Odd Fellows lodge. The degree was not materially changed between the time it was first used within an Odd Fellows lodge and its independent use in the Rebekah lodges, which indicates that the inclusion of the Chaplain was original.[18]

The Patriarchs Militant were developed in 1885.[19]  Unsurprisingly, the ritual included a Chaplain as the necessity of a Chaplain in the other branches had long been established by this point. Interestingly, although the Patriarchs Militant evolved from the earlier uniformed Encampments,

---

15. *1853 Digest*, Grand Lodge of the United States, (1854) p. 33

16. *Odd Fellows Monitor and Guide*, T.G. Beharrell (1888) p. 35

17. *The Odd Fellows Manual*, A. B. Grosh (1852) p. 75

18. *Odd Fellows Monitor and Guide*, T.G. Beharrell (1888) p. 35

19. *Odd Fellows Monitor and Guide*, T.G. Beharrell (1888) p. 396

the role of Chaplain in the Patriarchs Militant was invested in an appointed officer rather than included in the duties of a line officer. In this way, the Patriarchs Militant Chaplain resembles the Chaplain in the lodge more than the High Priest of the Encampment.

# The Role Across Branches

The role of the Chaplain is consistent across all branches, except in Encampment due to its nature as a combination of a Chaplain and an elected officer. However, it is worth noting the various similarities and differences of each branch to obtain a broader interpretation of the role of the Chaplain.

## Odd Fellows Lodge

While there is no portion of the Charge of Office for the Chaplain in our Odd Fellows subordinate lodge ritual, we can clearly understand what the role is envisioned to be by referring to the Installation ceremony. In that ceremony, the Chaplain's role is stated to be "to conduct the devotional exercises of your lodge and to perform such ritualistic work as appertains to your office. You are also to perform all duties the Order may enjoin."[1]

---

1. *Charge Book for an Odd Fellows Lodge*, Sovereign Grand Lodge (2004) p. 173

The open-ended last portion of that set of duties covers offering prayer at meals, offering support to members in distress, and any other duties needed to promote the health and harmony of the lodge. The various prayers and parts in degrees are provided in the Ritual, with additional ritualistic duties as defined in the auxiliary rituals and ceremonies that can be found in later chapters of this book.

# Rebekah Lodge

In the Rebekah lodge ritual, we have two references from which to draw the description of the Chaplain's duties. In the Charge of Office, the Chaplain does not have a described duty, but rather a general duty as expressed, "to live peaceably, do good unto all as we have opportunity and especially to obey the Golden Rule."[2]

While this duty is enjoined upon all members, it is the especial purview of the Chaplain. Similar to the Odd Fellows lodge, the Chaplain is instructed in the Installation explanation of duties "to conduct the devotional exercises of your lodge and to perform such ritualistic work as appertains to your office. You are also to perform all duties the Order may enjoin."[3]

The prayers and ritualistic duties are found with the lodge ritual and the auxiliary rituals and ceremonies in later chapters of this book. As with the Odd Fellows lodges, the additional duties of a Chaplain in the Rebekahs include offering prayer at meals, offering support to members

---

2. *Ritual of a Rebekah Lodge*, Sovereign Grand Lodge (2009) p. 19

3. *Ritual of a Rebekah Lodge*, Sovereign Grand Lodge (2009) p. 95

in distress, and performing any other duties needed to promote the health and harmony of the lodge.

# Encampment

Beginning with the Charge of Office, the High Priest has the duty to "counsel the members of the encampment to improve themselves in the lectures and charges, as well as in the practice of their doctrines; to conform to the general regulations, and thus preserve the uniform mode of working in this Encampment; and to give such instructions to newly admitted members as the good of the fraternity may require."[4]

The first part of that duty is similar to that of Chaplains in other branches, in which they also have a role in lectures and charges. The last portion is similar to the duties of other Chaplains regarding providing instructions during degrees.

It is interesting to note that, while the ritual includes prayers for the High Priest to perform, those are not specifically listed in the duties of the office. Even looking at the Installation ceremony, the duties of the High Priest do not specifically indicate any duty to perform prayers.[5] Yet such expectations do exist, as the High Priest is required to perform prayers in the rest of the Ritual.

The Charge of Office for the High Priest within Encampment does include duties to give "instruction to the uninformed" and be "active,

---

4. *Charge Book for an Encampment,* Sovereign Grand Lodge (1996) p. 15

5. *Charge Book for an Encampment,* Sovereign Grand Lodge (1996) p. 168

prudent and faithful". It also includes the wording: "Your office requires you to exemplify the unparalleled faith Abraham had in the command of God." This is perhaps the most explicit spiritual direction in the Order. In short, the opening statement of the Installation charge is very true when it says the High Priest's duties are "solemn and most interesting."

# Canton

Canton is the one branch in which there is no direct charge related to the duties of the Chaplain. There is no Charge of Office in their opening ritual and no Installation Charge.[6] Even more unusual, the Code of General Laws[7], which contains a line covering the duties of a Chaplain in every other branch, has no such language for the Patriarchs Militant. The role of Chaplain in the Patriarchs Militant is entirely undefined. As a result of there being no charge or definition unique to the Patriarchs Militant, the duties of the Chaplain can only be assumed to be similar to those of a lodge Chaplain.

# Junior Lodge and Theta Rho

The duties specified for the Chaplain in the youth branches of the Order do not deviate from the duties specified for the Odd Fellows lodge and

---

6. *Ritual of a Canton of the Patriarchs Militant,* Sovereign Grand Lodge (1997)

7. *Constitution and Code of General Laws,* Sovereign Grand Lodge (2003, revised 2024) XV

Rebekah lodge.[8]   That being the case, this Manual will not specifically discuss the youth branches further as the focus of the guidance provided in this work is directed towards adult members.

---

8. *Constitution and Code of General Laws,* Sovereign Grand Lodge (2003, revised 2024) XX.4H, XXII.4H

# GENERAL DUTIES

The Code of General Laws states, "The Chaplain will perform such duties as pertain to the office."[1]  By considering the role of Chaplain across all branches and examining the rituals and ceremonies, we can describe the general duties of the role.  These are grouped into three main categories: prayer, instruction, and leadership.

## Prayer

Throughout all of our rituals and ceremonies, there are prayers to be offered by the Chaplain.  In most cases, these prayers are specified, and the Chaplain must offer these prayers exactly as written in the ritual.  Standardized prayers in ritual serve to unite us, just as standardized text does for every other role in the ritual.  There are times for a Chaplain to

---

1. *Constitution and Code of General Laws,* Sovereign Grand Lodge (2003, revised 2024) VB.4H, VIII.13H, XX.4H, XXII.4H

offer a special and unique prayer for an occasion, and when that is the case, a Chaplain must remember that we are not of one religion.

It is inappropriate and against the rules of our Order for a Chaplain to offer a sectarian prayer during an official Odd Fellows event. For those who regularly attend the services of their own faith tradition, that can sometimes be difficult to remember. Beginning or ending a prayer in a manner that is ingrained in one's usual practice can be a hard routine to break, but break it we must.

There are two main reasons why. First, we do not all share the same faith traditions. Offering prayers in a sectarian style for one faith tradition excludes and even denigrates the faith of fellow members who follow another. That violates our rules that no member will be excluded from the equal enjoyment of our Order. Second, from a theological perspective, the Odd Fellows seek to invoke the protection, guidance, and mercy of the Supreme Being (in which we all believe as Odd Fellows), and we would fail in that effort if we offer a prayer to which any member retracts their individual blessing. In other words, if a prayer alienates the beliefs of a member, that member will not, in their heart, offer up that prayer, and we will not be united in invoking the protection, guidance, and mercy we seek.

As a Chaplain, it is an essential duty that your prayers unite all members in our common belief. In most cases, that is accomplished using the prayers prescribed in our rituals and ceremonies. In cases where there is no prescribed prayer, a Chaplain must demonstrate the strength of character to set aside personal preferences in style of prayer and offer up a prayer to which every member can give full assent. In the chapter entitled "Standard Prayers," you will find a collection of special prayers for various occasions that you may use when there is no prescribed prayer. In the chapter "Guidance of Prayers," you will find guidelines to assist you in developing any extemporaneous prayer you may be called upon to make.

# Instruction

A Chaplain is also a teacher. In our rituals, there are times when the Chaplain provides instruction about the lessons of our Order. In the Odd Fellows Initiatory Degree, the Chaplain explains the symbolic meaning of the various portions of the degree. While the charges and instructions from other officers contain important information and the work presented by the Noble Grand is essential to a member working in a lodge, they are often forgotten at the first hearing. What a candidate remembers most is the experience of the degree and the symbolic events that took place within it. Thus, it is the Chaplain's explanation of those symbolic events which, along with the events themselves, that are most remembered from the initial experience.

The Chaplain also serves as a teacher in various charges and lecture versions of the degrees in each branch of the Order. It is important to read through these portions of the ritual and familiarize yourself with them to fully understand your role in the lodge.

The Chaplain also takes the lead in providing the instruction for the Odd Fellows Memorial Day Service. In that ritual, the Chaplain instructs us in the meaning of the ceremony and general moral precepts. A copy of that ritual can be found in the appendices of this Guide.

# Leadership

A Chaplain is also a leader within the Order. This is not just limited to leading the members in prayer.

In the Third Degree, for example, it is the Chaplain who leads the other officers through the exposition of the symbols of Odd Fellowship. This is an extension of the role of the Chaplain as guardian and instructor of the symbolic side of Odd Fellowship.

The Chaplain also has a traditional role through custom and practice of providing calming leadership within meetings. While the presiding officer maintains order within the meeting, the Chaplain has long provided calming leadership through conciliatory statements and calls for respect and civility. Not being in charge of the debate, overseeing the funds of the body, nor the actions of committees, the Chaplain has a pseudo-outsider position during debates on issues within the body. Using that position to champion the tenets of Odd Fellowship rather than join in either side of a debate can greatly influence the tenor of the meeting and the harmony of the body.

The presiding officer must maintain order and sometimes make unpopular decisions, even if only with a portion of the membership. In times like those, a Chaplain can lead the body back to seeing its unity and higher purpose, becoming an invaluable asset to the Order.

Our Chaplains are not clergy and carry no special dispensation from any faith or creed. We function within a social tradition that views spiritual leaders as non-partisan. That inclination to look to and accept the guidance of a spiritual leader is both an opportunity and a responsibility for

Chaplains. Use it wisely to lead all members to uphold the principles of Odd Fellowship.

# FORM AND PRACTICE

The various speaking parts of the office of Chaplain are found in the Ritual for each particular branch of the Order and will not be replicated here. There are, however, forms and practices in performing those duties that are expected and are not explicitly stated in the Ritual. Those are covered in the following sections by branch of the Order to which they pertain.

## Odd Fellows Lodge

A chaplain should observe the key tradition in an Odd Fellows lodge: The Bible should be opened immediately before the opening prayer and closed immediately after the closing prayer.

The Bible should be placed at the Chaplain's station in the lodge, but a lodge that chooses to use the traditional altar in the middle of the room may place it there. If that is done, the Chaplain should approach the altar, opening the Bible, and then return to the Chaplain's station before reciting the opening prayer.

Likewise, after the closing prayer, the Chaplain should approach the altar and close the Bible before returning to that station. The tradition can be summarized as follows: when the Bible is open, the lodge is open.

When a lodge goes into recess, the Chaplain should close the Bible. When the recess ends, the Bible should be reopened. This long-standing custom ensures that no "profane" activities occur under the auspices of the lodge. The previously mentioned custom of the lodge being open when the Bible is open applies to this, as the lodge is not in session if it is in recess, and thus, the Bible should not be open during that time.

The Draping Ceremony was revised for the Manual of Instruction for Odd Fellows lodges. The full ceremony is included in the chapter entitled "Draping Ceremony." It is worth noting here that the Chaplain no longer leaves the Chaplain's station during the Draping Ceremony. The prayer is given from the Chaplain's station. However, for the Undraping Ceremony, the Chaplain is still escorted to the center of the room by the Warden and Conductor before the prayer and escorted back to the Chaplain's station after the drape is removed.[1]

# Rebekah Lodge

In the Rebekah lodge, there is a procession of officers to begin the meeting. The Chaplain should enter last, carrying a closed Bible on the

---

1. *Manual of Instruction for Odd Fellows Lodges*, Sovereign Grand Lodge (n.d.) p. 26-28

palms of their hands and placing it on the altar before falling into line. When the Noble Grand directs the officers to assume their stations, the Chaplain goes directly to the Chaplain's station.[2]

When the Noble Grand directs the Chaplain to invoke the Divine Blessing, the Chaplain should advance to the altar, open the Bible, bow the head, and cup the left hand in the right at about waist height. After the prayer, the Chaplain should drop the hands and proceed to the Chaplain's station, entering it from the right.[3]

For the closing prayer, the Chaplain should again advance to the altar, cup the hands, and bow as before. After the prayer, close the Bible and return to the Chaplain's station, entering on the right.[4]

If the lodge performs the Regalia March, the Chaplain will remain at the rear of the altar until the members begin singing "An Evening Prayer" (or some other song as designated by the Noble Grand). At that point, the Chaplain will retrieve the Bible and place it, closed, upon the palms of both hands, then proceed with the Warden and Conductor to the anteroom.[5]

The Draping Ceremony requires the Chaplain to pre-position the open Bible at the Chaplain's station. After the charter has been draped and the garlands placed, the Chaplain carrying the open Bible advances with

---

2. *Manual of Instruction for Rebekah Lodges,* Sovereign Grand Lodge (n.d.) p. 4-5

3. *Manual of Instruction for Rebekah Lodges,* Sovereign Grand Lodge (n.d.) p. 11

4. *Manual of Instruction for Rebekah Lodges,* Sovereign Grand Lodge (n.d.) p. 30

5. *Manual of Instruction for Rebekah Lodges,* Sovereign Grand Lodge (n.d.) p. 31-32

the Past Noble Grand to the altar. After the Past Noble Grand reads the resolutions, and the members sing "Blest Be the Tie that Binds", the Chaplain reads the first four verses of the Twenty-third Psalm, then closes the Bible and places it on the palm of the left hand. After the unison response, return to the Chaplain's station and re-open the Bible.[6]

# Encampment

In the Encampment, the High Priest should open the Bible immediately after the Chief Patriarch asks if the High Priest has formally assumed that station. The act of opening the Bible is the sign of formally assuming the station.[7]

Note: The Bible should be at the High Priest's station.

When it comes time for the closing prayer, the High Priest should close the Bible before proceeding to the center of the circle and giving the closing prayer.[8]

As you can see, the Encampment operates differently than the other branches. The Bible opens earlier than it does in other bodies and closes sooner.

# Canton

---

6. *Manual of Instruction for Rebekah Lodges*, Sovereign Grand Lodge (n.d.) p. 35-36

7. *Charge Book for an Encampment*, Sovereign Grand Lodge (1996) p. 10

8. *Charge Book for an Encampment*, Sovereign Grand Lodge (1996) p. 21

The Chaplain in the Patriarchs Militant should never wear a hat, sword, or gloves with the uniform. The lack of a sword speaks to the spiritual role of the office, and when a Chevalier is not in possession of a sword, they should not wear gloves. The lack of a hat is an interesting choice. Rather than simply uncover during prayers, the Chaplain remains uncovered at all times to symbolically indicate that service to the Supreme Being is not limited to times of prayer.

The Bible is opened prior to giving the opening prayer and kept at the Chaplain's station. The Bible is closed following the closing prayer.

Generally, the Chaplain does not fall into line for inspection and remains at the Chaplain's station to handle the Bible and perform the prayers. In a smaller Canton, the Chaplain may choose to participate in the formation of the Canton and, if done, will fall out of line to attend to the Bible and offer prayers from the Chaplain's station.

## Providing Comfort

There is a significant difference of opinion as to whether the Chaplain has a duty to the spiritual well-being of the members. To some, spiritual well-being is synonymous with general well-being, and they believe, therefore, that spiritual well-being is a valid duty of the Chaplain.

Others consider spiritual well-being as a personal matter that treads too far into the realm of sect or creed to be admissible within the bounds of Odd Fellowship. This Manual will not opine on that matter because it is not a point of consensus nor is it a point of historical precedent, law, or ritual.

While spiritual well-being will not be a part of the duties covered by this Guide, the general well-being of the members is undoubtedly within the duties of the Chaplain. That is so because the general well-being of our fellow members is the concern of every member, the Chaplain included.

The Chaplain, by the perception of the position, can have a more profound role in caring for our members and promoting their general welfare. The ways in which a Chaplain may perform those duties can be broken into three main areas: aiding the sick and distressed, providing guidance during Good of the Order, and taking an active role in helping members who are struggling.

# Sick & Distressed

One of the best ways to serve the welfare of your members is to serve on the Visiting Committee to make contact with and assist those members who are reported as being sick or in distress. As you are the visible point of connection between the members and their prayers, it is natural that those same members would take comfort from your presence, well wishes, and offering of prayers. It is also only natural that the members present at a meeting may expect you to have contacted members previously reported sick or in distress and to offer a prayer for their recovery.

In the chapter entitled "Standard Prayers," you will find prayers for those who are sick or in distress. You will also find prayers for thanksgiving when a member has recovered or at times when someone has a happy event to report.

# Good of the Order

Often, members report good news about themselves or others during Good of the Order. This is a perfect time to offer a prayer of thanksgiving, joining the members in a joint acknowledgement of the joyous event and reminding the members that as Odd Fellows we believe in the providence of a Supreme Being.

Good of the Order is also a wonderful time to share thoughts with the members to help bridge divides, promote harmony, and reinforce the teachings of the Order. These need not be long commentaries, but simply positive and harmonious observations. Just be mindful that when you offer these reflections that you do so using only the lessons of Odd Fellowship and not bring in additional material of a particular sect or creed. There really is no topic about which you would need to speak for which there is not already a clear lesson taught by our rituals and symbols to which you can refer.

# Members in Times of Difficulty

Perhaps the hardest job for any person, let alone for the Chaplain, is to provide meaningful support to members of their community who are struggling.

With the exception of trained professionals, we are not equipped to handle many of the deeper issues of mental health or severe personal difficulties. Those limitations should not discourage you from taking action.

A helping hand, an open heart, and a listening ear are often what is needed most. If you feel that there is a concern serious enough to warrant the involvement of professionals, it is your duty, as exemplified in the teachings of our Order, to take action to protect the well-being of that member.

Barring extreme cases where a member may cause harm to themselves or others, there are some practical methods for helping a member who is struggling so that you can effectively show support and suggest any applicable programs available to assist.

The key to being an effective support for others is adhering to the Golden Rule: Treat others how you would like to be treated. We have all experienced periods of distress of one type or another in our lives, and remembering how that felt can help guide you in treating others how you would want to be treated.

As a Chaplain, you may wish to comfort or support other members who are experiencing emotional difficulty. While you cannot act as a professional counselor, the following principles can help you provide compassionate support in a way that respects individual boundaries and promotes well-being. These are simplified from standard counseling guidelines[9] and modified to align them with the limitations of being a Chaplain.

Respect for Member Autonomy

- Every member has the right to make decisions about their own life, feelings, and actions. You can support them as you would

---

9. *ACA Code of Ethics*, American Counseling Association (2014)

want to be supported by encouraging them to make their own choices about handling their difficulties or seeking help. It is ok to offer ideas or resources, but avoid pushing for a particular solution. It is not your life or your problem, and you need to respect others' choices even if you would do things differently.

Empathy and Understanding

- Along with the Golden Rule, empathy is the ability to put yourself in someone else's shoes and understand how they feel. This is best accomplished by being an active listener. Look at the member as they talk, maintain an open posture, nod, and ask clarifying questions to show that you are trying to understand their experience rather than simply waiting to give advice.

Non-Judgmental Attitude

- Approach the situation by fostering an accepting environment by avoiding criticism or disapproval of the member's feelings or choices. Focus on their experience rather than your own opinions or judgments. If you disagree with their perspective, keep an open mind and remind yourself that everyone's circumstances are unique, and it is their choice.

Confidentiality

- Just as we do not discuss the lodge's business with outsiders, we do not discuss the personal communications entrusted to us. Do not share a member's personal problems or sensitive information with others unless they give you explicit permission to do so or there is a safety issue that requires immediate action, such as harm to themselves or others.

### Cultural Sensitivity and Competence

- Recognizing and respecting differences in background, culture, beliefs, and values is important. Ask questions if you are unsure and show openness toward the member's cultural viewpoints or traditions. Avoid making assumptions and remember that each person's experiences and beliefs shape how they experience distress and healing. In particular, as an Odd Fellow, remember to refrain from involving individual religious beliefs.

### Trust and Rapport

- Trust and rapport are built by building a supportive and reliable relationship where members feel comfortable sharing their thoughts and feelings. Be consistent in your interactions. If you promise to check in, do so. Show genuine warmth and honesty. Over time, these small acts build trust.

### Collaborative Approach

- Work together with the member to find ideas and strategies that might help them. Instead of telling them what to do, explore possible options together. It is ok to suggest options so long as you give the member the space to consider them and make their own choice.

### Boundaries

- Know the limits of your role. You are a volunteer, not a therapist or medical professional. Even if you are a therapist or medical professional in your private life, you're not in the Odd Fellows. Offer a listening ear and basic help, but recognize when to recommend professional services. Avoid taking on more than you can handle, and avoid becoming the sole source of support for someone with a very serious issue.

Self-Awareness and Self-Reflection

- Understand your own emotions, biases, and limits so that you can support others more effectively. Notice if certain topics or situations trigger strong feelings in you. Seek advice, mentorship, or self-care when you feel overwhelmed so that you can remain calm and helpful.

Ethical and Legal Standards

- Act in the best interests of the member you are helping while following all the relevant Odd Fellows teachings and Code. Be familiar with the rules of the Order and our teachings so that you stay within the bounds of Odd Fellowship. If someone is in immediate danger or discloses the abuse of a minor or vulnerable adult, report it to the proper authorities.

These basic principles all fall within the basic scope of the Golden Rule and the principles of Odd Fellowship. Remember that Friendship, Love, Truth, Faith, Hope, Charity, Fidelity, and Universal Justice cover almost every type of problem and form a strong foundation upon which to offer valuable support and guidance should you choose to be more involved in the well-being of your fellow members.

# Organizational Resources

It is also valuable for you to understand the resources and programs the Odd Fellows offers to assist its members in times of need. Each lodge should have a Relief Committee to address the needs of members, in addition to the Visiting Committee previously mentioned.

Jurisdictions also offer programs for the relief and benefit of members. These can range from assistance during emergencies to scholarships, medical cost aid, and many other areas. Be familiar with your jurisdiction's programs and look beyond your lodge, encampment, or canton for help.

The Sovereign Grand Lodge has a host of programs to help those in distress, with education, and with various medical issues. These resources are available to our members, and you should be familiar with them so you can offer them as options for members in need.

# Addressing Change

Across our Order, there are differences of opinion on many topics. That is certainly to be expected in any large and diverse group. We all believe in the core tenets and teachings of the Order despite any differences we may have on various details. During the preparation of this Manual, the opinions of various members across all branches were received and considered. The most significant issue raised relates to the prayers contained within our various branch rituals.

Some chaplains modify various prayers or omit the ritual prayer and replace it with a personally created prayer. Quite frankly, that is wrong.

It is understandable that any individual may feel that any particular part of our rituals should be changed. Rituals do change. However, there is a process by which those changes are made. As members of the Independent Order of Odd Fellows, we agree to abide by the rules and regulations of the Order. That includes faithfully performing the rituals, in full, in their authorized form.[1]

Changes may be needed. Those proposed changes must be submitted to The Sovereign Grand Lodge to be considered by the Committee on Ritualistic Work and then by the body as a whole. This is the process by which all members have a voice. It is disrespectful to the membership at large for any individual or lodge, encampment, or canton to unilaterally change the ritual based on personal preference. That is being a stick which has removed itself from the bundle, a link which has chosen to break the chain of connection.

As an Odd Fellow or Rebekah, and more especially as a Chaplain within the Order, it is your duty to uphold the rules of the Order and perform the authorized rituals as written. This is not just a duty for the sake of duty, but also a safeguard against creating new disharmony by inadvertently causing offense to those who share different beliefs or opinions from yourself. While the ritual may not be the perfect fit for every member's personal beliefs, it has the virtue of being the authorized form.

Consider the annual report form. How many members would like to see that form revised in some way or another? How many of those changes would be contradictory with one another? Where would we be as an Order if each lodge decided to report its membership and finances in its own preferred format or just to skip that report altogether? It would cause chaos and ultimately be destructive of the Order.

---

1. *Charge Book for an Odd Fellows Lodge*, Sovereign Grand Lodge (2003) p. iv

Changing or omitting portions of the ritual at will is no different. It is equally destructive of the Order. We have our core beliefs, our rules, and our ritual as the things that unify us as the Independent Order of Odd Fellows. If each member or local unit decided on its own what the beliefs, rules, and rituals are, then we would not be one united band.

The experience of a member should be, as far as beliefs, rules, and ritual are concerned, the same in one lodge as in another. A member should be free to travel from lodge to lodge and find a common tie in those areas and, through those, a sense of belonging. A member should not visit another lodge and feel like an outsider because the lodge is performing a ritual that is alien to that member.

If you believe that change is needed, please draft the changes you believe necessary and submit them for the consideration of The Sovereign Grand Lodge. If your proposals make sense to the majority of the Representatives from across our Order, then they will be adopted. In one's opinion, the will of the majority may not be the right choice, but it is the system under which we chose to belong and that we are obligated to obey.

# CONCLUSION

Being a Chaplain is not an overly complex responsibility. Most of what you need to know on a regular basis can be found in the standard ritual for each branch and in the supplemental ceremonies.

# STANDARD PRAYERS

## Blessing for a Meal

O God, our creator and preserver, we gather here in a spirit of Friendship, Love, and Truth. Bless the food we are about to share and grant us the wisdom to offer kindness and support to one another. May this meal bring nourishment to our bodies, fellowship to our gathering, and renewed commitment to serving our members and our community. In gratitude, we give thanks to you. Amen.

## Prayer for Sick or In Distress

O God, our creator and preserver, we lift our thoughts for our dear Brother/Sister _____ who is facing struggle. May the warmth of Friendship surround them, the power of Love uplift them, and the light of Truth guide them toward peace. Grant them comfort in body, mind, and spirit, and strengthen our resolve to support them with caring hearts and helping hands.  May they find hope, renewal and support through you.  Amen.

# Prayer of Thanksgiving

O God, our creator and preserver, we pause in thankfulness for the good news we have received.  May our hearts overflow with gratitude as we recognize blessings both seen and unseen.  Let our joy inspire us to share kindness with others and to continue building a community rooted in Friendship, Love, and Truth.  In gratitude, we lift our thanks to you. Amen.

# Benediction

O God, our creator and preserver, as we conclude this gathering, we do so in gratitude for the fellowship we have shared.  May the spirit of Friendship guide our words, the power of Love inspire our actions, and the light of Truth illuminate our path.  Go with us now, as we strive to carry these values into all we do and all we serve.  Amen.

# GUIDANCE ON PRAYERS

We are fortunate to have two excellent guides in our effort to develop prayers for special occasions. They come from two different times, but they explain the bounds within which a Chaplain should stay while preparing any prayer.

The first comes from the standard tract adopted by the Grand Lodge of the United States in 1867 entitled "Odd Fellowship – What is it?" which was written by the esteemed Ridgely:

> "Odd Fellowship is a moral, not a religious organization. The religious world is divided into many sects, each intent upon the promotion of its peculiar plans and interests, and of consequence wanting in that unity of action so essential in every secular institution to the securement of those great results which illustrate the triumph of *benevolence* and *charity*. This want is, in a good degree, met by the

employment of an agency not amenable to such a disability, and in which men of many *sects* and *creeds* may cordially co-operate and labor, upon common ground, for the relief of human suffering. Such an institution is Odd Fellowship. It does not array itself against the CHURCH, nor presume to arrogate its functions, or to supervise its teachings. Its lodges are not the council rooms of enmity to religious, civil, moral or social organizations. Far otherwise; all its oracles and instructions in relation to these grave subjects find their warrant and authority in the divine law, under the inspiration of which it proclaims the Golden Rule as the sublimest illustration of the law of love."[1]

Those beautiful words help guide the content and tenor of the extemporaneous prayers a Chaplain may be called upon to offer. They remind us to focus on the principles of Odd Fellowship and our common virtues.

The second resource comes from the 1888 Journal of the Sovereign Grand Lodge:

"Our Order only requires a belief in the existence of a Supreme Being as a qualification for membership, and has no affinity with any religious sect or system of faith; hence everything savoring of sectarianism is not to be tolerated. The words "systems of faith or sect" do not have reference

---

1. *Odd Fellowship – What is it?*, Grand Lodge of the United States (1867) as printed in *Book of Forms*, Sovereign Grand Lodge (1904) p. 254-255

merely to sects within the pale of Christianity, but have a far broader significance and include all the religions of the world.  In this sense, Christianity is a sect; hence it is inexpedient, unwise and unlawful to make a prominent reference to it in lodge work.  The S.G.L. in 1882, Journal 9147, adopted forms of prayer to be used in the opening and closing.  These forms were adopted to avoid the danger of offending brethren of different sects or systems of faith by one of opposite faith in extemporaneous prayer. If lodges follow these forms there will be no danger of offending, for although taken from the Christian Bible and including the Lord's Prayer, they exactly accord with the fundamental doctrines above referred to.  We have Jews and we may have Mahommedans and other non-Christian sects within our Order, and the rule applies to them equally with members of the Christian faith.  They would not be allowed to use in prayer words which would be offensive to Christian ears; hence it is better to avoid alluding to matters belonging to the particular faith of the Chaplain engaged in prayer."[2]

This wise instruction focuses not on the broad view of our purposes and beliefs as the previous instruction, but rather on not offending those who may not share our faith traditions.  Ask yourself if your prayer would be as equally welcome in a gathering of those who hold very different faith traditions than your own.  It does not matter if you believe every member in attendance shares your same faith tradition because that is

---

2. *1903 Digest*, Sovereign Grand Lodge (1904) p.505-506

not the point. The point is that your prayers as a Chaplain in our Order should be acceptable to all members of all faith traditions, whether present or not.

Remember, the All-Seeing Eye is always upon us, and we should constantly strive to treat other members as we would wish to be treated. This means respecting their faith traditions both before their faces and behind their backs. A prayer you give should be given as if every member in the Order will hear it, and should be acceptable to each of them.

# RELIGIOUS SYMBOLS

## The Bible

"The Holy Bible is an integral part of Odd Fellowship and is so regarded by the Sovereign Grand Lodge. It must be present at the Chaplain's station in every lodge while open for business. The Bible may be placed in other positions in the lodge-room during the conferring of degrees, at Memorial or Funeral Services, or at other lodge functions when deemed expedient."[1]

That statement adopted by the Sovereign Grand Lodge remains a true and binding statement to this day, but it is not a recent addition. The 1880 ritual adopted by the Sovereign Grand Lodge had it only slightly different: "The Holy Bible is an integral part of Odd Fellowship and is so regarded by the Sovereign Grand Lodge of the I. O. O. F., and it must be

---

1. *Charge Book for an Odd Fellows Lodge*, Sovereign Grand Lodge (2004) p. 33

present in every lodge while open for business."[2]   As mentioned earlier, the requirement for the Bible to be present at all times was adopted in 1878.[3]

The reason why the Bible in particular is an integral part comes from the earliest days of Odd Fellowship.  In the first adopted ritual from April 1820, in the "Making" of an Odd Fellow (what we today would call the Initiatory Degree), there is the following line, "Place your left hand upon this holy and sacred book, and your right hand upon your left breast, and repeat after me this solemn oath."[4]   After repeating the obligation, the candidate was obliged to "Kiss the book."[5]

The Bible was the object upon which oaths were taken in all manner of proceedings, and it was only natural that the same would be true in Odd Fellowship.  The role of the Bible expanded to be more than just the physical representation of the Supreme Being in whose name an oath was being given.  As the degree system evolved into the five-degree format existing prior to the Ridgely revisions, the Holy Bible was one of the symbols of the Fifth Degree.  As Ridgely himself writes of the degrees prior to his revision, "An hourglass is rapidly exhausting its sands, and a coffin stands ready for the bier; but above them with illuminated pages, is the open book of the oracles of God."  He goes on to explain them thus:

---

2. *The Independent Order of Odd Fellows' Ritualistic, Secret, and Floor Work* by F. Walker (1887) p. 16

3. *Digest*, Sovereign Grand Lodge (1903) p. 505

4. *Charge Book*, Grand Lodge of Maryland (1820) p. 11

5. *Charge Book*, Grand Lodge of Maryland (1820) p. 12

"For time flies rapidly away and the grave has its victory; but TRUTH never fails, and will endure forever."[6]

The Bible was equated in Odd Fellowship with Truth, and it has remained a symbol of the highest degree within the Odd Fellows lodge, even after the Ridgely revision to reduce the number of degrees. The Hourglass, Coffin, and Holy Bible remained the penultimate symbols of an Odd Fellows lodge and were joined by the Scales and Sword.

For Odd Fellows: "The Bible is an exhaustless fountain of truth, the storehouse from which all our principles are derived. Guided by its instructions, we may reach that golden age when the shackles of prejudice will be broken, the shackles of mental and moral bondage fall off, and man, redeemed and liberated from the slavish life of the passions, we will assert our high birthright, and own the ties which bind us in the universal relationship with our fellow man."[7]

Originally a physical representation of the Supreme Being within our initiatory ritual, the Bible became a symbol of Truth, and eventually the source of all our degrees and lessons. Could the Odd Fellows have found sources for the same lessons in other texts? Of course, we could have, but we did not build our Order on a different text.

Whether one believes in the divine nature of the Bible is irrelevant to whether the lessons we take from it are true lessons. That David was anointed by God to rule over the Israelites is not something an Odd

---

6. *History of American Odd Fellowship: The First Decade* by James L. Ridgely (1878) P. 503

7. *Charge Book for an Odd Fellows Lodge*, Sovereign Grand Lodge (2004) p. 141

Fellow must believe in order to understand and see the truth in the bond of Friendship between Jonathan and David expressed in the Bible. The same is true for all the other lessons derived from the Bible in Odd Fellowship in all the branches of the Order. There is no requirement to believe that the Bible was divinely written, just that it is the text from which our principles are derived and that those are true.

# Other Symbols

The prohibition against symbols that pertain to any particular faith or creed is repeated several times in the Code of General Laws and applies to flags, pictures, ornaments, other religious books, and any other item that could be interpreted as pertaining to a particular faith or creed. This prohibition does not apply to individuals who may wear symbols of their own faith on their person.

The prohibition applies only to the lodge or encampment. The membership of a lodge or encampment cannot authorize such a display, regardless of opinions on its suitability. A lodge or encampment may seek a dispensation to allow or a decision about the legality of an item. For lodges or encampments that meet within a building owned by a religious organization, in which symbols of a particular faith or creed are displayed, a dispensation should be requested to permit the lodge or encampment to operate under those conditions. Alternatively, the lodge or encampment could seek a decision to determine that the lodge or encampment is not exhibiting those symbols because they are exhibited by the building owner without the action or approval of the lodge or encampment.

## With regard to Odd Fellows lodges:

"Lodges may not exhibit in their hall or anteroom any symbols that pertain to any particular faith or creed; but may use music that is generally regarded as religious if it does not cause controversy."[8]

## With regard to Rebekah lodges:

"Lodges may not exhibit in their hall or anteroom any symbols that pertain to any particular faith or creed; but may use music that is generally regarded as religious if it does not cause controversy."[9]

## With regard to Unified encampments:

"Encampments may not exhibit in their hall or anteroom any symbols that pertain to any particular faith or creed; but may use music that is generally regarded as religious if it does not cause controversy."[10]

## With regard to encampments:

"Encampments may not exhibit in their hall or anteroom any symbols that pertain to any particular faith or creed; but may use music that is generally regarded as religious if it does not cause controversy."[11]

---

8. *Constitution and Code of General Laws,* Sovereign Grand Lodge (2003, revised 2024) IV.3B(2)

9. *Constitution and Code of General Laws,* Sovereign Grand Lodge (2003, revised 2024) VII.3B(2)

10. *Constitution and Code of General Laws,* Sovereign Grand Lodge (2003, revised 2024) X.1(25)

11. *Constitution and Code of General Laws,* Sovereign Grand Lodge (2003, revised 2024) X.2(25)

# DRAPING CEREMONIES

## Odd Fellows Lodge & Encampment

### CEREMONY FOR DRAPING THE CHARTER

*Note: Each lodge shall determine the place where the Charter shall be placed for the draping ceremony, where the Charter shall stay while draped, and how long it shall remain draped. (The period used by many lodges is thirty days.)*

*Where the titles of Noble Grand, Warden, Conductor and Chaplain are used in the Odd Fellows lodge, the titles of Chief Patriarch, Junior Warden, Guide and High Priest shall be substituted in the Encampment.*

*At the time designated for the Draping of the Charter, the Noble Grand shall call up the lodge and address the members as follows:*

**Noble Grand:** "Brothers and Sisters of [here state lodge name and number], the angel of death has once more descended upon our beloved Order. This time the call has come for [Brother(s) / Sister(s)] [name or names], who [was or were] taken from our midst on [date or dates]. It is most fitting that we assembled here to pay tribute to [his/her or their] memory by the draping of our Charter. Our Warden and Conductor shall place the Charter of this lodge in position for the draping ceremony and then receive the drape from the Noble Grand and place it upon our Charter."

*Note: As the Warden and Conductor start to carry out the instructions of the Noble Grand, appropriate music shall be played. The music shall continue until the Charter is draped. The music should become very soft as the drape is placed upon the Charter and stop completely when the Warden and Conductor step back from the Charter. When the Charter is draped the Warden and Conductor shall stand before the Charter in reverent attention.*

**Noble Grand:** "Let us unite with our Chaplain in prayer."

**Chaplain:** Almighty God, who makest no life in vain and who lovest all that Thou hast made, lift upon us the light of Thy countenance and give all Thy comfort. We pray Thou will keep in tender love the spirit of our departed brother/sister, whose life we shall hold in blessed memory. Help us who continue here to serve Thee with constancy, trusting in Thy promise of Eternal Life, that hereafter we may be united with our brothers in the glory everlasting. Amen.

*The Noble Grand seats the lodge.*

# CEREMONY FOR UNDRAPING THE CHARTER

**Noble Grand:** Warden and Conductor *(these officers rise)*, you will place the Charter in the center of the floor, and then escort the Chaplain to the center of the floor, next to the Charter. *(Chaplain facing Noble Grand.)*

**Warden:** Noble Grand, your orders have been obeyed.

**Noble Grand:** Let us unite with the Chaplain in Prayer. *(Noble Grand calls up the lodge.)*

**Chaplain:** Our Heavenly Father, we come into thy presence to thank thee for the wonderful assurance, which you have given us, that through belief, though dead, yet shall we live; and whosoever believeth, shall never die, and while on Earth through our belief we live with thee and when death doth come, we enjoy eternity with thee.

We would ask that thou always aid and support our humble efforts to learn and practice the lessons of *friendship, love* **and** *truth.* And when we also will lay aside our mortal bodies, that we shall be accepted into thy kingdom. This we would ask in thy Holy Name. Amen.

**Noble Grand:** Warden and Conductor, you will remove the drape. This concludes the Ceremony of Un-Draping the Charter in Memory of Brother/Sister _____.

*Warden and Conductor, escort the chaplain to her station, and then place the Charter in its proper position.*

*Noble Grand seats the lodge.*

# Rebekah Lodge

## CEREMONY FOR DRAPING THE CHARTER

*When the Charter is to be draped, all things should be placed in readiness before the lodge is opened. Easel, holding charter, at Altar facing the Noble Grand's station. Drape and candles at station of Noble Grand. Garlands of flowers at station of Vice Grand. Resolutions at the station of the Past Noble Grand, and the Bible at the station of the Chaplain.*

*Officers taking part are Noble Grand, Vice Grand, Conductor, Warden, Chaplain, Past Noble Grand, Musician and the Supporters of the Noble and Vice Grand.*

**Noble Grand** (*Under "New Business"*)**:** Sisters and Brothers, once more the hand of death has entered our Fraternal Circle and removed from our midst one of our members, Sister/Brother _____. Let us pause at this time to pay respect to our member by draping our Charter.

*Noble Grand lights tapers.*

*Soft music. At chord all officers taking part rise together.*

*The Noble Grand calls up the lodge.*

*Noble Grand and Vice Grand step to positions in front of their respective stations. Noble Grand holding tapers and charter drape on arm; Vice Grand holding spray (or sprays) on extended palms.*

*Warden and Conductor face each other, march together and face the Noble Grand. Noble Grand presents tapers to Warden and Conductor, who receives them and carries them with both hands, partially extended. Warden and Conductor turn backs together, step out in line with sides of Altar, and march slowly to Altar, turn and face Altar and reverently deposits tapers on corners of Altar. Warden and Conductor step back two paces facing sides of Altar.*

*Noble Grand and Vice Grand, acting together, step about two paces forward, then each, turning slowly about, face their own stations. The Supporters of the Noble and Vice Grand step down to positions directly in front of their chairs, face each other, march together and face the Noble and Vice Grand respectively. The Noble Grand deposits drape on inside arm of her Supporters, who carry drape on palm supported by other hand. The Vice Grand deposits spray or sprays on arms of her Supporters. Noble and Vice Grand each turning right, return to their respective stations.*

*The four Supporters then march forward, slowly and reverently to Altar. Supporters of Noble Grand place drape on charter. Supporters of the Vice Grand place garlands on Altar. All step back two short paces, facing Altar.*

*The Past Noble Grand, carrying resolutions and Chaplain carrying open Bible, advance slowly to the Altar, taking places in line with the Warden and Conductor.*

*The Past Noble Grand reads the Resolutions.*

*All members sing one verse of "Blest Be the Tie that Binds".*

Blest be the tie that binds.

Our hearts in threefold love;

The fellowship of kindred minds

is like to that above.

*The Chaplain reads the first four verses of the Twenty-third Psalm.*

*Chaplain slowly closes the Bible, resting it on the palm of her/his left hand.*

*All incline heads and in unison say:* "Thy will O Lord, not ours be done."

*All turn and walk very slowly to stations.  Seated together.*

# Funeral Service

## FUNERAL SERVICE
## FOR THE USE OF LODGES AND ENCAMPMENTS

*When used by Encampments, the necessary changes in titles, etc., must be observed.*

*The lodge will assemble in the lodge room or in such other place as shall be designated by the Noble Grand in the call which he/she shall issue for the ceremony.*

*Each lodge should have a regular funeral team consisting of an Acting Noble Grand and Acting Chaplain. Each member of this team should be able to read well and correctly so as to avoid the embarrassment of halting and poorly read passages, and the mispronunciation of important words. For instance, the word immortality should not be pronounced immorality as has sometimes been done to the embarrassment of the relatives, friends and members of the lodge.*

*Emblems of mourning worn by members of the lodge shall be uniform, and may be either a band of crepe on the left arm or a black badge on the left breast.*

*The lodge will form in the regular order for processions. If the distance is not too great the lodge will march to the place of service. Otherwise the members will fall out and ride to the place of service, where they will re-form the procession.*

*If the service be held in the lodge room, or within any other building, the Noble Grand and Chaplain shall stand at the head of the casket as nearly as practicable, the Noble Grand on the right and the Chaplain on the left side. The members shall remain in front of the casket and in a body so far as convenience will allow but never between casket and relatives.*

*If the service be held at the grave the Noble Grand and Chaplain shall stand at the head of the casket as nearly as practicable, the Noble Grand on the right and the Chaplain on the left side. The members will stand in a group near casket.*

*Provision shall be made for the near relatives of the deceased to occupy a place in view of the casket. The rights of all members of the family of the decreased member should be fully respected, especially during the period of bereavement and, if at all possible, and where desired, they should be allowed full view of the ceremony, being very careful and considerate in not standing between members of the family and remains of the deceased member.*

*Appropriate music may be used at any time, as the Noble Grand shall direct.*

*Any portion of this ceremony may be given at the lodge room, the home or any other suitable place, and the remainder of the ceremony shall be given at the grave. This shall be determined by the Noble Grand according to the circumstances of the case.*

*When the officers and members are in their places the ceremonies shall begin.*

**Noble Grand.** — My brothers and sisters, we have assembled to perform the last service the living can render to the departed: to pay respect to one to whom we were bound by the claims of sincere friendship, unfeigned love and simple truth, one who was born as we were born, who lived as we now live, and who for many days enjoyed his/her possessions, power and friendships. When we lay to rest his/her earthly remains, we will cherish a lively recollection of his/her virtues.

**Chaplain.** — Let us Pray, Our Father, in this hour of sorrow, we turn to Thee for help. Thou gavest life, Thou hast received it unto thyself again. May the lesson of this hour sink deep into our hearts and purify them. May friendship and love take new meaning in our lives, and may Thy truth guide us by righteousness to Thee. Comfort all whose hearts are made lonely at this hour. Assure them of Thy presence, and in their sorrow teach them to know that Thou hast received the spirit of their loved one to Thyself again. Amen.

**Noble Grand.** — Often have we been reminded in the solemn ceremonies of our Order of the great truth that all that is born must die. How cheerless the home of the dead when unrelieved by the prospect of immortal life! But hope remains over man's last resting place like an arch bright with life everlasting (*immortality*), which, based upon earth, extends far into the sacred realms of eternity.

When the hour of death comes, it is faith in this immortality that brings consolation. Though we part, never to meet again on earth, yet do we feel that somewhere, somehow, we shall rejoin our brothers and sisters. We look forward to a time when with clearer vision, we shall know them in forms that never fade, in states that never change.

Today, we are in the full realization of health and enjoyment of the pleasures of this world. In a little while, the ever burning furnace of time will consume to ashes all that hath life and vigor in this terrestrial sphere.

Once, but surely once, will come to every one the call that takes a soul from earth. We bow in love and in humility to the will of God. The Chaplain will now present a lesson from that storehouse from which all our principles are derived.

**Chaplain.** — Lord, Thou hast been our dwelling place in all generations. Before the mountains were brought forth, or even Thou hadst formed the earth and the world, even from everlasting to everlasting. Thou art God.

Blessed is the man that walketh not in the counsel of the ungodly, nor standeth in the way of sinners, nor sitteth in the seat of the scornful. But his delight is in the law of the Lord; and in His law doth he meditate day and night. And he shall be like a tree planted by the rivers of water, that bringeth forth his fruit in his season; his leaf also shall not wither; and whatsoever he doeth shall prosper.

*If for any reason it is deemed advisable, the Chaplain may read such additional Scripture as he/she shall deem appropriate.*

**Noble Grand.** — His/Her life span has ended. The light of his/her eye has gone out; and his/her lips are forever silent. His/Her toils and labors are done. The burning taper of life has been extinguished and he/she has crossed the silent river of death.

[Optional: "My brothers and sisters, you are aware of his/her contribution to our beloved Order. No more will his/her counsel be heard within our lodges, yet his/her wisdom will continue to aid us in our work. No more will he/she labor with us; yet the results of his/her labors will continue through years that are to come."]

His/Her work among us is done; yet his/her influence will live to direct our actions for the good of our Order. We will miss him/her from our midst; but we will ever remember our associations with him/her; and we will keep ever in mind the obligations that we owe to those who were near and dear to him/her.

*Here may be given such further remarks as the Noble Grand shall deem appropriate.*

**Noble Grand.** — As a token that the virtues of our brother/sister will forever dwell in our memories we deposit this evergreen upon his/her casket.

*The Noble Grand deposits the evergreen and as he/she does he/she repeats the words:*

**Noble Grand.** — Farewell, Brother/Sister, until we meet thee in the Eternal Home.

*[Optional: The Vice Grand will lead the procession, followed by the Chaplain to pay their respects to the deceased member and continue around the room to their original position. Each member will repeat the words: "Farewell, Brother/ Sister" and at the same time will deposit the evergreen.]*

**Noble Grand.** — As a token that the virtues of our brother/sister will dwell greenly in our memories, we deposit this evergreen upon his/her casket.

*The Noble Grand deposits the evergreen and as he/she does so repeats the words:* "Farewell, brother/sister, until we meet thee in the Eternal Home."

*To be followed by the same or similar procedure as above.*

**Noble Grand.** — Brother/Sister was initiated an Odd Fellow in _____ Lodge No. _____, of the Grand Jurisdiction of _____ on the _____, _____. He/She became a Past Grand of _____ Lodge.

*Here fill in such history of the deceased member's full connection with the Order as is appropriate.*

At the time of his/her death he/she was a member _____ Lodge No. _____.

**Noble Grand.** — The mortal remains of our brother/sister will be laid to rest within God's earth from whence he/she came.

**Chaplain.** — Let us Pray, Almighty and Supreme Ruler of Heaven and of Earth, look down, we pray Thee, with compassion upon this scene; give peace and comfort to these bereaved and give to us the strength to live the obligations that we owe to them. Bless our Beloved Order here and everywhere. May Friendship, Love and Truth be not unmeaning words upon our lips, but the sentiment of our hearts and the practice of our lives. May we live Thy law; the law that commands us to do unto others as we would that they should do unto us, and, when, after a life well spent on earth we shall pass through the valley of the shadow of death, and cross the silent river to join our loved ones gone before, may we meet Thee, Our Father, and hear the welcome plaudit, "Well done, good and faithful servant, enter into the joy of Thy Lord."

God of the Universe while we entrust the spirit of our departed brother/sister to Thy Holy care, may the record of his/her virtues be inscribed upon our hearts and his/her memory cherished by us forever. And we further pray in the words of Thy servant of old "The Lord bless us and keep us. The Lord make his face to shine upon us and be gracious unto us evermore." Amen.

# GRAVESIDE CEREMONY

*Upon all occasions the canton/encampment/lodge may turn out in full dress uniform or regalia. If the deceased has been a member of the Patriarchs Militant there may be an Honor Guard post if requested and there are the required number of members to participate.*

**Noble Grand.** — We meet here today with hearts full of sorrow and grief to perform the last service which the living can render to the dead; to pay respect to our beloved Chevalier to whom we were bound by sincere friendship and true love and whose memory with us will always be a sweet benediction of peace. Let us pray.

**Chaplain.** — Most Gracious Father, in this hour of sorrow, we turn to Thee for help. Thou gavest life—Thou hast taken it away. In the midst of life we thus often are brought face to face with death. Help us, O God, to realize that, though permitted to tarry for a short time, we are hastening toward eternity. Help us to feel that we neither live nor die to ourselves, that Thou dost spare us for a purpose. We thank Thee for the Christian's hope—a hope that reaches beyond the tomb; and while Thou has removed from us our beloved [Chevalier, Brother, Sister], we thank Thee that we do not mourn as do those who are without hope—the hope of a better world—a world where life and immortality are brought to light through Thy word. Graciously grant us grace of Thy presence on this solemn occasion and Thy blessing upon us in the further solemnities of this hour. Help us to glorify Thee on Earth that we may all be reunited at last in Heaven. Amen.

**Noble Grand.** — _____, _____ [name and rank(s)], united with _____Lodge No. ____ I.O.O.F. on ____ of _____ ____ and answered the Master's last call on ____ of _____ ____. The immortal Ruler of the Universe has called him from his labors on this earth to an exalted position in the Heavens above. The burning taper of his life has been extinguished and he has crossed the silent river of death. The light of his eyes has gone out and his lips are forever silent. Although his face will be hidden from our vision and his voice will no longer be heard, his virtues, his fidelity and his noble deeds are indelibly engraven upon our hearts and our memories forever. His hands were full hands, as well as busy hands. He sought not only to make conditions better, but to make life sweeter and happier. He raised the tone of life and gave himself to the service of those around him. In all gratitude we can say of him that we are happier because he lived, that we are better because his life touched ours, and because of this we and all with whom we come in contact are made better and happier and a beneficent influence has resulted. As there comes to us the thought of lives cut short in the midst of usefulness, let us heed for ourselves the lesson that it taught. If life be short and death so sure, how can we be so careless of the lives we live or the death we die? Waste not the hours so precious and so fleeting. Work while the day of life may last so that, after life, we shall still be in the hearts and love of those we have blessed by the kindly words and deeds. Let us bow in humble submission to Him who has taken from our midst our beloved [Chevalier, Brother, Sister] and friend, who, though dead, speaketh and bids us to meet him midst those celestial joys, which "*Eye hath not seen, ear hath not heard, nor hath it entered into the heart of man to conceive*". "*Blessed are they who die in the Lord.*" Let us pray.

**Chaplain.** — Almighty and Supreme Ruler of Heaven and of Earth, we pray Thee to look with compassion upon this scene; give peace and comfort to these bereaved ones; remember them in mercy and give them patience under their affliction. Guide and direct us in all things. Bestow Heaven's benediction upon us all and help us to glorify Thee on earth that we may all be reunited at last in that heavenly home above. The Lord bless us and keep us; the Lord make His face to shine upon us and be gracious unto us. The Lord lift up his Fatherly countenance upon us and give us peace, now and evermore. Amen.

# MEMORIAL DAY SERVICES

CEREMONY FOR MEMORIAL DAY SERVICES
FOR DECEASED MEMBERS OF THE I.O.O.F.
AUTHORIZED BY
THE SOVEREIGN GRAND LODGE
SEPTEMBER 1894
(GENDER REVISED, 2025)

*Officers process into the site of the memorial and face audience.*

*HYMN.*
Air — *"America" or recited as a poem by a designee.*

> We sing our honored dead.
>
> And on their tranquil bed
>
> Proud tribute fling;
>
> Here let our song arise,

Like incense to the skies,

A living sacrifice

To them we sing.

No voice of woe shall wreathe

Amidst the strains we breathe

With grateful breast;

Theirs was a work well done.

Theirs was a race well run.

Theirs was a victory won

Of peace and rest.

**Prayer by Chaplain.** — Our Heavenly Lord! As we thus gather may we be imbued with the joyful spirit of thankfulness for Thy many mercies, as well as with solemnity for this hour's devotions.

We remember Thy goodness to us all the days of our life. Give us this day an ear for the orphan's cry, and the widow's woe. Help us to live that we may be worthy followers of those who have passed on before. May be learn our duty to the living as well as proper reverence for the dead.

Let Thine eye be open to all our needs, and Thine ear quick to attend our every cry until we follow our Brethren to that land where all tears are wiped away. We ask in His name.

Amen.

**Noble Grand [Grand Master].** — In accordance with the laws of the Independent Order of Odd Fellows, we have assembled today as Odd Fellows to pay loving tributes of respect to the memory of our deceased

Odd Fellows, who, one year ago were with us, but now have passed beyond the veil.

An enlightened and civilized nation reveres the memory of its dead, and it is fit and proper for all people sometimes to lay aside the cares of life, and wend their way to the silent cities of the dead, to drop the loving tear and strew flowers of Spring upon their graves. And so, we, as members of this great fraternal institution, today meet, that our dead may not be forgotten, but that their virtues may be mad known and their memory kept green.

Since our last Memorial Day, many of our Brothers (and Sisters) have departed; their voices are hushed – their chairs are vacant, their last battle has been fought, their warfare has ended, and peacefully they have sunk to rest. I thus call upon you, my Brothers (and Sisters), that we may fittingly spend this time in commemorating their good deeds and be fitted, when we go hence, to emulate their virtues and be ourselves prepared for the great change that awaits us all.

*The Secretary may now read a roll of the deceased and, if desired, suitable biographical sketches or if done at a memorial site, the Noble Grand or Grand Master now places the wreath.*

**Chaplain.** — My Brothers and Sisters, most solemn thoughts have pervaded our every mind, as you recollected our members who, one short year ago, aided us in these sweetly sad exercises. Some of them were then in their full glow of health, and were ambitious of further success and usefulness in this world – but they were cut down.

Long may they live in our memory and their bright examples be unto us beacon lights to guide us in the work of Odd Fellowship. In the sharp conflicts of opinion, the heat of debate, may their hallowed memories hush every unkind word and discordant thought and span the storm of controversy with the rainbow promise of peace and love. Sitting at the feet of their shadows, let us treasure the legacy they have bequeathed as a sacred trust, beautified, adorned, and enriched by their added sacrifice.

Death is the one event that comes to every human being. From real or imaginary evils, we may, in the Providence of God, escape; in this conflict, however, there is no retreat; there is no departure from this world of sin, sorrow, and suffering, to the higher and diviner life, but through the gates of death. Neither tears nor anguish, nor breaking heartstrings can avail anything when the fatal summons comes; they are utterly powerless to ward off the grim messenger. All we can do is to bow before the great affliction, and reverently say: "The Lord gave and the Lord has taken away; blessed be the name of the Lord."

The All-Wise Ruler of the Universe has given unto us to know good and evil, and right from wrong, so that we are thus forewarned and forearmed against the possible moral dangers that can accrue to weak humanity, and prepare against that day of reckoning which surely awaits all mankind. Our life here should be made a time of careful and steady preparation – as by our deeds we shall be justified or condemned in that great day.

Friendship fostered in our hearts becomes transformed into the golden chain of Love, which binds us firmly together upon the immovable rock of Truth, the foundation not only of our glorious Order, but of all things that are good and abiding.

Duty properly performed, becomes a pleasure to the doer, as well as of lasting benefit to the one aided. Our days are numbered and our end we know not.

"That solemn day will surely come,
The appointed hour make haste;"

And we must all go to face the record of our deeds.

May we, therefore, so live with the approval of our conscience and our God, that, whenever we are called, we may enter joyfully the Grand Lodge above.

*HYMN.*
Air — *"Boylston" or recited as a poem by a designee.*

"It is not death to die,
To leave this weary road;
And with the Brotherhood on high,
To be at home with God.
"It is not death to close
The eye long dimmed with tears,
And wake in glorious repose
To spend eternal years.
"It is not death to hear
The stroke that sets us free
From dungeon chain to breathe the air
Of boundless liberty."

**Prayer by Chaplain.** — Our Father, so guide us in accordance with these godly admonitions, that we may be taught so to number our days that we may apply our hearts unto wisdom.

May we early learn to look only to Thee, the Author of everything good and perfect, and with Thine approval, so live while here, that in the world to come we may have life everlasting.

Pass by our imperfections, forgive our misdoings, cheer us by Thy presence when we come to enter the Valley of the Shadows, and bring us to Thyself in Heaven for His Name's sake.  Amen.

*Officers process out.*

# Decoration Day Ceremony

CEREMONY FOR DECORATING THE GRAVES
OF DECEASED MEMBERS OF THE I.O.O.F
AUTHORIZED BY
THE SOVEREIGN GRAND LODGE
SEPTEMBER 1894
(GENDER REVISED, 2025)

*Officers process in to the graveside and face audience.*

**Noble Grand [Grand Master].** — My Brothers and Sisters, before we proceed with the duties of the day, and place over the remains of our departed friend(s) the floral tributes we have brought, let us invoke the Divine blessing.

**Chaplain [Grand Chaplain].** — O, Thou Great and Eternal God, our Father, Creator, and Preserver of the Universe, look down and bless us in the solemn services of this day.  Wilt Thou give grace to emulate the virtues of Brothers and Sisters sleeping beneath the silent sod?  And while we pay our tribute to their memory, may we never forget that reverence for the dead is best shown by care for the living.  Bless the widow and the orphan; and raise them up kind friends in the hour need.  And may we, together with our departed Brothers and Sisters, gain admittance to the Celestial Lodge above – there to be with Thee forever.  Amen.

**Response.** — Amen.  So may it be.

*The procession will then place the wreathes/flowers at the grave(s) and repeat one of the following selections – different ones can be used at different graves.*

SELECTIONS:

1. The memory of the just is blessed.

2. After life's fitful fever he/she sleeps well.

3. Love casts a garland on the grave that may not blossom more.

4. Thou hast now thy crown of flowers, take now thy rest.

5. Lives such as theirs build their own monument.

6. Peace is the just person's memory; let it grow greener with years and blossom through the flight of ages.

**Noble Grand [Grand Master].** — Brothers and Sisters, we have now performed the duties of the day, and by these simple services have paid a tribute of respect to those of our number who have finished their life on earth.  Our Order, instituted for purposes of self-help, and calculated to aid its members in the struggles incident to life, does not allow death to terminate the fraternal relationship formed within our ranks. After we have carried our deceased members to their last resting place in the silent city of the dead, they still retain a claim on our affections. Through their bereaved and orphaned family, they still ask our sympathies, and our material aid; and while they have themselves passed beyond the need of those kindly benefactions we owe each other in life, they still hold a place in our memory and love.

We stand today by the graves of our Brothers and Sisters who have gone to their rest. Some has reposed beneath the sod for years and their names are almost forgotten by the world. Some have but lately been laid in their silent bed, and warm hearts are still grieving over their death. But for all alike, in sorrow and in love, we have come to awake the tender thoughts of old associations – to recall to mind the virtues of our departed friends – and to lay on their graves the floral offering that shall speak for us, better than words can speak.

Silent are our departed Brothers and Sisters now; but could their voices come from beneath our feet, for each one of us would they utter this solemn exhortation:

> "So live that when thy summons comes to join
> The innumerable caravan that moves
> To those mysterious realms, where each must take
> His chamber in the silent hall of death,
> Thou go not like the quarry slave at night,
> Scourged in the dungeon; but sustained and soothed.
> By an unfaltering trust, approach the grave

Like one who wraps the drapery of his couch
About him, and lies down to pleasant dreams."

**Chaplain [Grand Chaplain].** — Almighty God, our Heavenly Father, we pray Thee to accept this humane service performed on memory of those whose loss we mourn. May we be enabled to emulate their virtues, and meet them again in that land where the links of friendship are not broken by the hand of death. Amen.

**Response.** — Amen. So may it be.

**Chaplain [Grand Chaplain].** — The Lord bless you can keep you. The Lord make His face to shine upon you, and be gracious unto you. The Lord give you peace. Amen.

**Response.** — Amen.

*Officers process out.*

# ANNIVERSARY OF THE ORDER CEREMONY

## ANNIVERSARY OF THE ORDER CEREMONY

*If the meeting be of the membership alone, in the lodge-room, then the regular opening ceremonies shall be gone through with, and such other business transacted as may be necessary, which being done, the Noble Grand shall commence the services of the day/evening as follows:*

*If the meeting be a public one, the above directions will be dispensed with, and the Noble Grand, having called the meeting to order, shall say:*

**Noble Grand.** — Brothers, Sisters (and friends), we are assembled to observe the anniversary of the forming of our Order [and The Sovereign Grand Lodge]. Without Divine recognition and direction, all our efforts and observances fail of success. Be devoutly observant, therefore, while the Chaplain shall invoke the blessing of the Supreme Ruler upon this meeting.

Prayer by the Chaplain. *(All rise.)*

**Chaplain.** — Almighty and ever-living God, our Universal Father and Common benefactor, from whom cometh every good and perfect gift; Who art lavish in blessings upon us, and without Whom nothing can prosper, we beseech Thy presence with us, and Thy benediction upon us, as we are here assembled. Graciously direct the aim and spirit of this gathering. Shower Thine abundant favors upon us. Let the words of our mouths and the silent admonitions of our hearts, while we wait before Thee, be acceptable in Thy sight, O Lord, our strength and our inspiration. Amen.

**Noble Grand.** — Vice Grand, why this convocation of Brethren, and for what object are we assembled?

**Vice Grand.** — Obedient to the Proclamation of our Sovereign Grand Master and the Proclamation of our Grand Master, we have now convened that we may gratefully render, as is becoming our due sense of gratitude, devout thanksgiving to Almighty God, for His abundant love and preserving mercy, and that we may further fittingly commemorate the (_____) anniversary of the founding of our beloved Order [and of The Sovereign Grand Lodge its (_____) year].

**Noble Grand.** — Brother Secretary, you will please read the Proclamation of the Sovereign Grand Master, and also the Proclamation of the Grand Master.

*Secretary reads as directed.*

**Noble Grand.** — Vice Grand, where and when had American Odd Fellowship its beginning? [When was The Sovereign Grand Lodge organized?]

**Vice Grand.** — In the city of Baltimore, in the State of Maryland, on the 26th day of April, in the year 1819. That was a memorable day, of which this is an anniversary. [The Sovereign Grand Lodge separated from the Grand Lodge of Maryland the 15th January 1825 in the city of Baltimore, Maryland.]

**Noble Grand.** — Who were its founders and first advocates?

**Vice Grand.** — Thomas Wildey, John Welch, John Duncan, John Cheatham and Richard Rushworth.

**Noble Grand.** — Had these Brothers been previously affiliated or connected with Odd Fellowship?

**Vice Grand.** — They had. They were formerly members of the Order in England.

**Noble Grand.** — Where did they meet to organize the first American lodge?

**Vice Grand.** — At the house of William Lupton, sign of the Seven Stars, Second Street, Baltimore.

**Noble Grand.** — Whence did these Brothers obtain a Charter for the organization of a lodge?

**Vice Grand.** — The Charter was obtained from the Duke of York's Lodge, of the Manchester Unity, Preston, England. This Charter was not received and formally adopted until the 23rd day of October 1820.

Previous to this time the first organized American lodge existed as a social beneficent independent Body.

**Noble Grand.** — What was the name given to the first lodge of American Odd Fellows?

**Vice Grand.** — The name chosen was Washington, a name dear to every American patriot, and a name today and forever honored and revered throughout the civilized world.

**Noble Grand.** — Has this lodge continued its existence under its original English Charter?

**Vice Grand.** — No. On February 22, 1821, Washington Lodge No. 1, surrendered its English Charter to its Past Grands, who then organized the Grand Lodge of Maryland and of the United States. Subsequently and immediate to the organization of this Grand Body, it re-chartered Washington Lodge No. 1.

**Noble Grand.** — What were the objects of these pioneer Brethren, whose names and memory are so precious to all lovers of humanity, in founding Odd Fellowship in America?

**Vice Grand.** — Those declared in all our Charters, viz.: "For the aid and protection of Brothers when in sickness and on travel, and for the purposes of benevolence and charity."

**Noble Grand.** — Was there any special rule laid down for the Order's guidance in the furtherance of this work?

**Vice Grand.** — Yes. It is contained in the legend on the Seal of The Sovereign Grand Lodge, which legend is the mandate of the Order: "We command you to visit the sick, relieved the distressed, bury the dead, and educate the orphan."

**Noble Grand.** — Was this rule intended to apply to men of any particular party or creed?

**Vice Grand.** — No; it is comprehensive as the human race. It rises above party, sect or creed. Here all the believers in the one living and true God may unite in the bonds of a universal Brotherhood.

**Noble Grand.** — Is it intended either to supersede or to supplement creeds, beliefs, or ordinances in matters of religion?

**Vice Grand.** — By no means. It assumes no prerogative of the spiritual. Its members are free and untrammeled in all that lies between God and themselves. It interferes with no duty which they of conscience, owe to God, their country, their families or themselves. It is a minister only to man's temporal needs. It seeks but—

> To meliorate the sorrows of mankind,
> Relieve the poor, the sick, the maim, the blind;
> Lift up the drooping heart; the widow cheer,
> And wipe away the helpless orphan's tear.
> To form of men one wide-spread Brotherhood
> Linked only in the bonds doing good.

**Noble Grand.** — What has been the influence and result of this Order upon its associated membership and in the general community?

**Vice Grand.** — It has developed the social being of the individual life, broadened man's appreciation of the true value of his brother man, and has made man, under the teachings of the principles of Friendship, Love, and Truth, a more noble son, a more devoted husband, a more excellent father and a better citizen.

**Noble Grand.** — What has been the growth and development of this Order?

**Vice Grand.** — It has expanded into a fellowship that is unbounded by territorial limit or language. In various nationalities it has been organized and into different tongues its Ritual has been translated. Its beneficent and helpful work is known and practiced throughout the civilized world.

**Noble Grand.** — How has this marvelous progress been accomplished?

**Vice Grand.** — Solely upon the merit of this noble fraternity, under the agency and fostering care of its various Grand and subordinate lodges, augmented by the personal efforts of its members in presenting and exemplifying to society its benign and helpful effects.

**Noble Grand.** — What have been, historically, the steps leading up to this interesting extent of our Order?

**Vice Grand.** — The organization of Washington Lodge No. 1, April 26, 1819; the Grand Lodge of the State of Maryland and of the United States, February 22, 1821; the separated Grand Lodge of the United States, January 15, 1825; The Sovereign Grand Lodge, September 18, 1879; as also the establishment of all our various Grand and Subordinate Lodges wherever extant.

**Noble Grand.** — Has the Order been true to its mission, and have its labors been crowned with success?

**Vice Grand.** — Its work has been achieved with manifest imperfection, but with uniform faithfulness. It has been constantly and helpfully aggressive. It has increased its membership until the little pioneer band has become a vast and influential army, influential in all that pertains to man's social betterment. Millions have been expended in its ministrations, and its accumulated. millions yet remain for the carrying on of its well-begun work. Under its humane agency the weary sufferer has been cheered by the presence of his sympathizing Brethren; material help, as a covenanted right, has blessed the stricken home; the widow and the orphan, in their solitude and need, have gratefully acknowledged its beneficence. By it, man has been drawn closer to his brother man; sorrow untold has been alleviated in the past, and it is gathering strength for its work in the years to come. It has increased in excellence as it has grown in age. Gloriously has it prospered, and its various agencies of helpfulness have been crowned with most abundant success.

**Noble Grand.** — It is, then, my Brethren, meet that we devoutly recognize the Divine guidance vouchsafed to us as a Brotherhood. We should fail of true gratitude if we did not continually praise and thank our Common Father for His great blessing in raising up and prospering our honorable institution. Especially on this anniversary day, so auspicious in the annals of our Order, it is most fitting that we come trustfully and reverently before the great God with heartfelt thanksgiving, for the development and extent to which our noble fraternity has grown; to praise Him for the good He has enabled us to do, and, with hearty acknowledgment of His hand in all our success, our progress, and our improvement, to rejoice before Him, and ascribe to Him all the honor and glory. Let us ever praise Him; let us never forget to thank Him for the past; let us constantly implore the continuance of His protecting care and ever abundant blessing.

*Here may be sung either of the following hymns, or such other appropriate music as may be selected. Or, it is competent for the lodge or committee, in providing for an anniversary observance, to introduce, at intervals, in this prescribed service such music as they may choose, providing it is not inconsistent with the Ceremony as here arranged.*

THANKSGIVING HYMN.
Tune — *"Coronation."*

All glorious mighty Lord, to Thee,
Our grateful song we raise;
Blest source of our prosperity,
Thy guardian care we praise.
Our Order, once a little band,
In weakness and in fear
Besought the guidance of Thy hand,
Its thorny path to cheer.
The few, through Thy preserving care,
Are now a mighty host;
And Thou, who hearkened to our prayer,
Shall be our constant boast.
Oft mid despondency and tears,
Our weary feet have gone;
But Thou, through long, eventful years,
Hast safely led us on.

## ANNIVERSARY HYMN.
Tune — *"Old Hundred."*

Father of love! Whose tender care

Has kept us through another year;

With tuneful voices now we raise

Our hearts to thee in grateful praise.

For mercies past, for joys to come,

For health, and happiness, and home,

For friendship pure, for love and truth,

That crown our age and cheer our youth.

Accept our thanks, our labors bless,

And to our efforts grant success;

And to Thine honor we will raise

Unceasing hymns of prayer and praise.

**Noble Grand.** — Fully realizing the blessing of Almighty God in the growth of our Order, let us all reverently turn our hearts unto Him in thanksgiving, while our Chaplain shall lead us in prayer.

**PRAYER.** *(All rise.)*

**Chaplain.** — O, Thou who rules in Heaven, and does Thy will amongst the inhabitants of the earth; Thou, the Lord God, infinite in all Thy perfections, glorious in Thy holiness, wonderful in all Thy works; we acknowledge Thee, as thou hast revealed Thyself, as the source of life and of every blessing, and we come before Thee with our offering of praise and thanks giving for the goodness and mercy with which Thou hast crowned our days. We recognize Thy wonder-working arm in the prosperity our Order has achieved, and we would, in gratitude, recall to mind the blessings Thou hast vouchsafed to us. With reverence we render thanks to Thee for the blessing which has come through this Order to the family of man. We thank Thee for its stately proportions and growth to such eminent usefulness to humanity, and for its constant influence in advancing the unity and helpfulness of the various races of the world. Whose hand but Thine has led us? Whose power but Thine has sustained us? Whose eye but Thine has watched over us? Thou, and Thou only, hast shaped our ends and directed our steps, and hast made our once feeble few to be as a nation in numbers, and hast made us most potent for good. For what we are by Thy favor, we bless Thee; and we pray Thee mercifully to forgive whatever we have done amiss. For all that we may yet hope to achieve, we ask Thy special guidance; we can accomplish naught without Thy favor. Graciously direct, in all the days to come, every avenue of effort of our beloved Order. Be our guide and shield in the future as Thou hast been in the past. Divest our Order of everything contrary to Thy will; prevent it from ever dishonoring Thy great name; direct it in its efforts to benefit mankind; make it successful in doing good; mold it according to Thine own pleasure, and may the family of man be blessed by its ministrations, and thus may Thy name be honored. Make us wise to see and faithful to improve our opportunities for doing good. May we have strength to obey Thee, and grace ever to honor Thee, and may the day soon come when all the nations, tongues and kindreds of the earth shall learn and do Thy will, and the whole family of man acknowledge Thee as their Lord, and be bound together in the ties of a universal Brotherhood. Grant this, O, Lord, and whatever else Thou seest best for us, and ultimately bring us, by Thy gracious favor, to the full fruition of life in Thy eternal kingdom, and unto Thy name will we ascribe all honor and glory, now and forevermore. Amen.

*Here should follow an oration or appropriate address; or, in lieu thereof, the Noble Grand or some deputized qualified member may read an address, the "Odd Fellowship – What is it?", or extracts from "The Objects of Odd Fellowship."*

*After this the following may be sung, or such other appropriate music may follow as shall have been selected:*

ODE — OUR BANNER.
Tune — *"My Maryland."*


Fling wide our banner! Land nor sea
Boast prouder gonfalon than ours;
It points to higher destiny
Than crowns the strife of mortal powers.

Chorus.
* Its field of white, its border bright,
Its links, denoting Union's might,
It waves, an angel's wing, above,
Proclaiming Friendship, Truth, and Love.

Wave, banner of the triple tie,
In tranquil glory o'er the land;
No dismal or ensanguined dye

Shall mar the folds that here expand.
It e'er shall share the brother's prayer,
The orphans rescue from despair;
A benison each wave shall fling,
And many a widowed heart shall sing.

Chorus.
* Its field of white, its border bright, etc.

May blessings ever on it rest,
While heralding our Order's fame;
In every motion manifest
The principles of good we claim;
Whose beaming ray shall round it play
Till merges in the night our day,
And other generations prize
The flag that greets our failing eyes.

Chorus.
* Its field of white, its border bright, etc.

**Noble Grand.** — We will be dismissed with the Benediction by the Chaplain. *(All rise.)*

**Chaplain.** — Now unto Him who is able to keep you from falling, and to present you faultless before the presence of His glory with exceeding joy, I commend you and the whole family of man; and to Him, the only wise God, our Lord, be glory and majesty, dominion and power, now and forever. Amen.

# Dedication of a Lodge Hall Ceremony

### FORM OF DEDICATION
### OF AN ODD FELLOWS' HALL OR LODGE-ROOM
### ADOPTED BY
### THE SOVEREIGN GRAND LODGE
### OF THE
### INDEPENDENT ORDER OF ODD FELLOWS
### REVISED 1924
### (GENDER REVISED 2025)

*This ceremony may be performed in the presence of a general audience, or in a lodge-room, with closed doors. If others than members are present, the honors will be omitted, and the Grand Officers will enter in due procession, and take their appropriate seats. If admission is restricted to members of the Order, a lodge will be first opened in due form and the*

*Guardians stationed at the doors. The Grand Lodge Officers, properly clothed, will form in another apartment, and approach the outer door, at which the Grand Herald will give the usual alarm.*

**Outside Guardians.** — Who comes there?

**Grand Herald.** — The Grand Master and other officers of the Grand Lodge of _____ who desire to be admitted in the name of Friendship, Love, and Truth, for the purpose of dedicating this Hall to the uses of the Independent Order of Odd Fellows, the diffusion of Benevolence and Charity, the inculcation of Fidelity and the exaltation of Universal Justice.

**Outside Guardian.** — Enter, in the name of Friendship, Love, and Truth.

*The same dialogue will occur at the inner door, with the Inside Guardian, after which the Grand Lodge Officers, except the Grand Marshal and Heralds, will enter the room and take their respective seats. If the dedication be in a Lodge-room, with closed doors, the honors of the Order will be given at the proper time.*

*The Grand Officers, except the Grand Marshal and Heralds having entered and taken their respective chairs, the Grand Master, after some introductory remarks, requests the brethren to rise and unite in singing the opening ode.*

ODE.

Brethren of our friendly Order
Honor here asserts her sway,

All within our sacred border
Must her high commands obey.

Join, Odd Fellowship of brothers,
In the song of Truth and Love;
Leave disputes and strifes to others,
We in harmony must move.

Honor to her courts invites us,
Worthy subjects let us prove;
Strong the chain that here unites us,
Linked with Friendship, Truth and Love.

In our hearts enshrined and cherished,
May these feelings ever bloom—
Failing not when life has perished,
Living still beyond the tomb.

**Grand Master.** — The Grand Chaplain will now address the Throne of Grace.

**Grand Chaplain.** — Direct us, O Lord, in all our doings with Thy most gracious favor, and further us with Thy continual help; that in all our works, begun, continued, and ended in Thee, we may glorify Thy holy name, and finally, by Thy mercy, obtain everlasting life. Amen.

**Grand Master.** — The brethren will please be seated.

*Grand Marshal and Heralds here enter. If possible let them be robed with turban, robe, and sandals, after the Eastern custom; that of the Herald of the North being white, of the South pink, of the East blue, of the West scarlet, and that of the Marshal, or Chief of the Heralds, royal purple trimmed with green and gold.*

**Grand Marshal.** — Grand Master, is it your will and pleasure that the ceremony of dedicating this Hall to the business and purposes of Odd Fellowship do now proceed?

**Grand Master.** Such is my will and pleasure.

*If the dedication be not public, the following, to and including the form of the altar, may be omitted.*

**Grand Marshal.** — Perhaps around no one thing in human history have the thoughts of man clustered with more of interest and reverence than around the altar. Before it all nations have bowed. At its sacred shrine all have worshiped. Here all sects and creeds, however divergent in faith, have offered their most hallowed sacrifices. An Eastern tradition tells us that the first man was made upon an altar—which God himself had prepared for that purpose—and that both the Patriarchs and King Solomon erected theirs on the same spot where this one stood. Whether from this tradition or otherwise the solemn reverence for the altar sprang, certain it is that everywhere and in all ages, whose records have come down to us, the hallowed associations of the altar have formed the great central attractions in all worships.

The Targumists tell us that Adam built an altar after he was driven from the Garden of Eden, and that on this altar Cain and Abel, and after them Noah and Abraham, offered sacrifice. The first authentic account, however, of an altar, is that of the one built by Noah after leaving the ark, in commemoration of that wonderful deliverance Altars were first erected on some spot hallowed by some great event or sacred association. Later they were erected on some eminence and were called "High Places". But wherever erected or for whatever purpose, whether for sacrifice or memorial, they have, in all ages, commanded the most profound reverence. Moved by this universal sentiment, Odd Fellowship has her altar—her sacred shrine—around and before which we, as Odd Fellows, bow and worship taking possession of this beautiful temple which is about to be solemnly dedicated to the ennobling principles of our Order, no further ceremony should or can lawfully proceed until we build our altar.

Grand Heralds of the North, the South, the East, and the West, are all things now in readiness?

**Grand Heralds.** — They are.

**Grand Marshal.** — Grand Herald of the North, where mountain and valley are perpetually robed in crystalline white, as purity of life and conduct is the first tenet of our Order, without which no one can become a true Odd Fellow, bring forth and place as the base of our altar a white stone—white being the universal emblem of *Purity*.

*Herald brings in a representation of a white stone, with the word "Purity" painted on the face of it.*

**Grand Marshal.** — And may our lives be as pure and spotless, and our integrity as firm and unyielding as the material of which it is composed. The next principle we meet in our onward progress is Friendship the emblematic color of which is *Pink*.

**Grand Marshal.** — Grand Herald of the South, the glow of whose genial warmth bedecks all nature with beauty and fragrance, giving to life new impulses and to development grander growth, bring forth and place upon this base the symbol of *Friendship*—that with which the ancients represented the warmth and ardor of youth.

*Herald brings in a representation of a pink stone, lettered "Friendship", and places it on the base.*

**Grand Marshal.** — It has been hallowed in poetry as typical of the spring-time of life Interwoven, by the great Architect of Nature, in every beam of light, as one of the seven primary colors; when disentwined by the power of the prism from its sister rays, it is found to possess the warmest glow and bends least from a straight line. This teaches us that our friendship should be ardent and true, and by no circumstances be turned from a worthy brother. Heed well its admonition.

**Grand Marshal.** — Grand Herald of the East, whence the rising sun sweeps from earth the gloom of night, and bathes nature in the beams of the morning—bring hither thy treasure, *Love*, the central link in our welded three, whose emblematic color is *Blue*.

*Herald here brings in a representation of a blue stone lettered "Love", and places it on the last.*

**Grand Marshal.** — How deeply significant. Blue is everywhere and universally the synonym of true. When this ray falls upon the polished steel, that steel acquires polarity and becomes a magnet, ever pointing unerringly "to its mysterious attraction in the chambers of the north".

Thus every brother, like the polished steel, when brought under the influence of the principles of our Order, becomes, or ought to become, so filled and permeated with love and good-will toward his fellows, that, like the magnet, he shall be sure a guide to the struggling, careworn mariner amid the fiercest storms of life.

Last in the triple link comes *Truth*, that imperial virtue fitly emblemed by *Scarlet*.

**Grand Marshal.** — Grand Herald of the West, sitting on thy throne of glory, as

> "Twilight lets her curtain down
> And pins it with a star—

Bring forth thy treasure, *Truth*, robed in the crimson hues of thy most glorious setting.

*Herald brings in a representation of a scarlet stone, lettered on its face with the word "Truth".*

**Grand Marshal.** — Place it upon the altar. *(Herald places it there.)* Symbol of glory, rank, and power, it is worn not less by Priest than King. Out of it Moses was commanded to make a garment for Aaron, and it formed a part of the robe, the ephod, the curious girdle, and the breast-plate of Judgment.

How beautifully appropriate this color to the completed character of the true Odd Fellow! See to it well, my brothers, that no one bearing this high distinction wears it unworthily.

Leaving the lodge we now ascend still higher to the Encampment Branch. Here cluster virtues more *ethereal*, if not more excellent. *Faith, Hope, Charity,* daughters of Heaven, fairest of celestial visitants, in this sanctuary, upon this altar of Odd Fellowship, let thy names be inscribed.

**Grand Marshal.** — Grand Heralds of the North and South, *Faith* in ever-living green shall bloom, symbol of Nature's universal livery, upon which the eye resting never tires.

*Heralds here bring in a representation of a green stone, lettered with the word "Faith", and place it.*

**Grand Marshal.** It points us to that undying trust, which, when the body crumbles, lights the valley of shadows. Planted on the rock of Truth, it shall spread its never-fading verdure along life's thorny pathway, cheering the despondent, and bearing up, as on eagle's pinions, the fainting, sinking, careworn child of toil.

**Grand Marshal.** — Grand Heralds of the East and West, now in golden beams let *Hope* appear and spring the rainbow arch of promise from out the falling tears of life's weary pilgrimage.

*Heralds bring in a representation of a gold-colored block or stone, lettered with the word "Hope", and place it.*

**Grand Marshal.** — Buoyed up with Hope, we will struggle on mid darkest hours, guided by that golden rule, "Whatsoever ye would that others should do to you, do ye even so to them." So, when we near the verge of the dark valley, as brightest day goes out in golden sunset, may it be ours to sink to rest amid Hope's brightest visions of golden promise.

Now abideth Faith, Hope, and Charity, but the greatest of these is *Charity*.

**Grand Marshal.** — Grand Heralds of the North and South, the emblematic color of this noblest of the graces shall be royal purple.

*Here Heralds of the North and the South bring in a representation of a purple stone, lettered with the word "Charity", and place it.*

**Grand Marshal.** — Type of highest rank and power, it comes freighted with earth's richest treasures. It brings to man the highest earthly good. It spans the River of Death. Radiant with celestial light 'tis the symbol of "The Brotherhood of Man, the Fatherhood of God, everywhere proclaiming as it goes, peace on earth, good-will towards men".

**Grand Marshal.** — Passing from the Encampment, we contemplate with admiration the Rebekah Degree, that great department of Odd Fellowship in which are enrolled the women of the Order, through whose loving deeds and gentle ministrations Charity finds its tenderest expression.

**Grand Marshal.** — Grand Heralds of the East and West, another pink stone, with that emblematic color, placed here in our altar, will typify *Fidelity*, even as its rays, when the dawn uplifts itself to kiss the new-born day, and its glow at evening when the shadows lengthen, are constant reminders of the Faithfulness of God's Covenant "While the earth remaineth, seedtime and harvest, cold and heat summer and winter and day and night shall not cease".

*Heralds of the East and the West here bring in a representation of a pink stone, lettered with the word "Fidelity" and place it.*

**Grand Marshal.** — Fidelity to the ideals of the Rebekah Degree gives to woman her sweetest charm; therefore let this stone rest here to her honor and the glory of her deeds.

**Grand Marshal.** — Grand Heralds of the North, the South, the East and the West, as we based our altar upon a white stone of *Purity*, so let us now crown it with another white stone, typifying that *Universal Justice* which the Chevaliers of the Patriarchs Militant, the highest branch of our Order, have pledged themselves to uphold and defend.

*Here Heralds join in bringing in a representation of a white stone, lettered with the words "Universal Justice", surmounted with an altar railing painted white, and place it—completing the altar.*

**Grand Marshal.** — Thus stands our completed altar, embodiment of the grand principles that underlie the stupendous fabric of Odd Fellowship. Today we assemble in the name of our Order to set apart and dedicate to these ennobling virtues, this edifice—*Purity, Friendship, Love, Truth, Faith, Hope, Charity, Fidelity, Universal Justice*, rising in climactic beauty, form a golden chain strong enough to link the world to the noblest and best that life affords.

'Tis fitting that the dedicatory ceremony should now proceed.

*Grand Marshal directs to be sung or rendered such ode or music as shall have been selected for the occasion.*

*The Noble Grand, President of the Hall Association, or Chairman of the Building Committee, will then step forward and present the keys of the Hall to the Grand Master, and say:*

Grand Master, we meet you here to-day to announce that the work in which we have been engaged is finished, and our Temple is at last ready to shelter us within its walls It is not the business of the committee to allude to their own labors, nor the manner in which those labors have been performed; nor would good taste permit them to descant on the fitness of our edifice for the sacred purpose to which it is designed. It is capable of speaking for itself through its proportions and its style. If these fail to impress you, any words of mine would prove worse than useless. I have only to repeat that our work is finished, and in behalf of _____ Lodge No. ____, and of the Order in this place, I make request that this Hall be set apart and dedicated to the business and purposes of Odd Fellowship

**Grand Master.** — Noble Grand [or Mr. President of Odd Fellows' Hall Committee]: in the name of, and in behalf of the Independent Order of Odd Fellows of the State/Province of _____, I accept, for dedication to the uses of Odd Fellowship, this Hall which has been constructed under your supervision. To you and your associates the present must be an occasion especially gratifying. To-day you witness the consummation of that for which you have zealously and faithfully labored, and to-day you behold the recognition, by your brethren from the North, the South, the East, and the West, of this, the result of your efforts, as a Temple devoted to the service of those whose vocation it is to visit the sick, relieve the distressed, bury the dead, and educate the orphan—duties which neither interfere with nor supersede the discharge of any other, social, moral, or religious.

Brethren! I congratulate you upon the completion of this beautiful Hall, which we are about to dedicate to those cardinal virtues which should adorn and elevate humanity, and the names of which we have selected as a motto and watchword of our beloved Order. Beneath this roof you are to encourage one another in the duties of benevolence and charity; before the altar the good works of Friendship, Love, and Truth are ever to be presented as the only acceptable sacrifices. From hence, as from a perennial fountain, are to flow the gentle streams of true Friendship, to gladden and make green many waste places In this quiet retreat are to be cultivated those flowers that Love unfeigned shall scatter on the rugged pathway of life, under many bleeding feet. Here is to be sown the good seed of Truth in many hearts, to spring up and yield its hundredfold harvest. It is, therefore, not so much this Temple made with hands that should occupy our attention at present as the great principles that are here to be disseminated. I hope and trust, brethren, that our united efforts, with those of our brethren throughout the globe, may lead to the raising and adorning of a still nobler Temple, which shall be consecrated by the approval of the Supreme Grand Master of the Universe, without the invocation of whose blessing no work should be undertaken.

The brethren will now rise and unite with the Grand Chaplain in prayer.

**Grand Chaplain.** — Almighty God, the maker of all worlds, whom we are taught to approach and coil by the tender name—Father; we would humbly draw near and beg Thy blessing on the work in which we are engaged. Whatever is amiss in us, do Thou make right by Thy Divine Power, and in all things do Thou overrule our thoughts and deeds to Thy greater glory and the good of our fellow-men. Amen.

*The following or other appropriate Ode or Anthem may be sung, or omitted.*

DEDICATION ODE.
Air — *"Cephas".*

"In Thee we trust!" the builders said,
And deep in earth they sunk the wall;
In Hope the corner-stone was laid,
And raised the building over all.
No accident has marred our trust—
No loss of life drawn forth regret—
Complete our Hall, it is but just
That it to Thee we dedicate.

Here may we with Fidelity
In Covenanted Love relieve
And Friendship with Remembrance be,
Till Truth her sovereign power give;
May Hospitality here reign
With Toleration's kindly Love,
And Faith each pilgrim soul sustain,
Until we reach Thy Tent above.

"In Thee we trust!" and thus to Thee
We offer all—for all is Thine!—
That Thy co-workers we may be
On earth in word and work divine.
When brethren want or death lays low—

When orphans cry in helpless youth—
When widows weep in cheerless woe—
Oh, Grant us "Friendship, Love and Truth."

**Grand Master.** — The brethren will be seated,

**Grand Master.** — I was glad when they said unto me; Let us go into the house of the Lord.

**Grand Warden.** — Our feet shall stand within thy gates, O Jerusalem.

**Grand Master.** — Jerusalem is built as a city that is compact together (at unity in itself).

**Grand Warden.** — Whither the tribes go up, the tribes of the Lord, unto the testimony of Israel, to give thanks unto the name of the Lord.

**Grand Master.** — For there are set thrones of judgment, the thrones of the house of David.

**Grand Warden.** — Pray for the peace of Jerusalem; they shall prosper that love thee.

**Grand Master.** — Peace be within thy walls, and prosperity within thy palaces.

**Grand Warden.** — For my brethren and companions' sakes, I will now say, peace be within thee!

**Grand Master.** — Because of the house of the Lord our God, I will seek thy good.

**Grand Warden.** — So be it.

**Grand Master.** — Hear! hear! hear! all men: By the authority and in the name of the Grand Lodge of the Independent Order of Odd Fellows of the State/Province of ____, I dedicate this Hall to the business and purposes of Odd Fellowship, to the dissemination of Friendship, Love, and Truth, to the diffusion of Benevolence and Charity in their fullest extent to all its worthy members to the inculcation of Fidelity and the exaltation of Universal Justice, and by this *(uplifted hand)* solemn act, I hereby declare it to be duly dedicated.  The Grand Marshal will please cause this dedication to be appropriately proclaimed.

**Grand Marshal.** — Brothers/Sisters, Grand Heralds of the North, of the South, of the East, and of the West: By the solemn act of the Grand Master of the Grand Lodge of _____, this Hall is duly dedicated to the business and purposes of Odd Fellowship, to disseminate Friendship, Love, and Truth, Faith, Hope, and Charity, in their fullest extent, to all its worthy members, to the inculcation of Fidelity and to the exaltation of Universal Justice.  It is his will and pleasure that the same be proclaimed, which duty you will now perform.

**Herald of the North.** — Hear all men by command of the Grand Master, and in the name of Friendship, as pure, refreshing, and life-giving as this water *(sprinkling it)*, I dedicate this Hall to the practice of that ennobling virtue, which, uniting men as brethren, teaches them to sustain that relation at all times, each in his turn helping and helped, blessing and blessed.

**Grand Warden.** — Behold how good and how pleasant it is for brethren to dwell together in unity; for there the Lord commanded the blessing, even life evermore.

*Here the following is allowed:*

CHOIR.
Air — *"Coronation"*.


      All hail the power of Friendship's name,

      Let every brother hail!

      Till Friendship's power and Friendship's fame

      Shall 'round the earth prevail.


**Herald of the South.** — Hear all men: By command of the Grand Master, I proclaim this Hall dedicated to Love, world-wide and ever enduring *(lights the fire on the altar)*, and may the fire that is this day kindled upon the altar of our hearts be as perpetual as that which burned upon the altar in the secret tabernacle of the Most High, of which this is but a feeble emblem.

**Grand Warden.** — Though I speak with the tongues of men and of angels and have not Charity, I am become as sounding brass or a tinkling cymbal. Charity never faileth.

*Here the following is allowed:*

CHOIR.


      All hail the power of Love divine,

      Our second, sweetest link;

'Round every heart her tendrils twine
And at her fountains drink.

**Herald of the East.** — Hear all men: By command of the Grand Master, I proclaim this Hall dedicated to the inculcation of Truth *(scattering wheat)*, and may the good seed here sown, of which this is the emblem, like the grain sown broadcast on the earth, spring up again an hundred-fold, for future use and blessing, and may that ennobling virtue which lies at the foundation of all other virtues, and which is devoid of guile and hypocrisy, teach us sincerity and plain dealing in all our communications, and earnestness in the inculcation of whatever is good and true.

**Grand Warden.** — He that walketh uprightly, and worketh righteousness, and speaketh the truth in his heart, O Lord, shall abide in Thy tabernacle and shall dwell in Thy holy hill.

*Here the following is allowed:*

CHOIR.

All hail the power of regal Truth!
Hail her with voice and deed!
Hail her strong men and sturdy youth
A friend in every need!

**Herald of the West.** — Hear all men: By command of the Grand Master, I proclaim this Hall dedicated to Faith, Hope, and Charity, Fidelity and Universal Justice.  Those graces, like these flowers *(strewing flowers)*, fill the common air with fragrance, beautify and adorn all on whom they fall. The practice of these highest virtues is in itself the fulfilling of that law which commands us to visit the sick, relieve the distressed, to bury the dead, and to educate the orphan.

**Grand Warden.** — A good man showeth favor and lendeth; he will guide his affairs with discretion; he hath disbursed; he hath given to the poor; his righteousness endureth forever; his horn shall be exalted with honor.

*Here the following is allowed:*

CHOIR.


All hail! our glorious Trinity!
Our battle-cry and creed,
Our potent three in unity!
They must and will succeed.


**Rebekah Matron** *(dressed in white)*. — Hear all men: By command of the Grand Master, I declare this Hall dedicated to Fidelity, as perfect and unchanging as the stars in the heavens, and as strong and unyielding as earth's foundation stones; and pledge the Rebekahs to ever assist in holding the word constantly before the world as emblematic of their constancy and devotion, for it is said of the true Rebekah,

"In fidelity and gentleness
Her spirit walks from day to day
Along the toiler's quiet way.
The hours to beautify and bless."

May all the influences that flow from this hall be as pure and spotless as the lily. *(Here the Rebekah Matron will place a lily on the altar.)*

Grand **Warden.** — Those who would succeed in life's battles must regard Fidelity with favor.

CHOIR.

"All hail the power of Fidelity,
Let all the sisters hail.
'Till purity's power and Friendship's name
Shall round the earth prevail."

**Chevalier/Lady** *(in full dress uniform).*—Hear all men in the ceremonies incident to the building of this altar and crowning it with the emblem of Universal Justice, it is fitting to say,

"Justice, Thou of Heavenly birth,
Come down and dwell upon the earth."

And by command of the Grand Master, I declare this hall dedicated to Universal Justice, and as emblematic of the intent and purpose of the Militant Branch of the Order, I place this sword upon the altar to be removed and wielded for defense of right and justice whenever occasion demands. *(Here chevalier/Lady will place sword upon the altar.)*

**Grand Warden.** — While traveling over hill and through valley the Protector is always ready to draw his sword in the name of Universal Justice.

CHOIR

"Be true to right; let justice still
Her even balance claim;
Unawed, unbribed, through good and ill
Make rectitude your aim."

**Grand Marshal.** — Grand Master. Proclamation has gone forth to the four quarters of the globe that all men may hear and know that Odd Fellowship has here a dwelling-place.

**Grand Master.** — The brethren will rise and the Grand Chaplain will address the Throne of Grace.

**Grand Chaplain.** — We humbly beseech Thee, O God, to bless the work in which we have now been engaged. Let the lessons we have received sink deep into our hearth, so that this shall have been to us no idle ceremony, but a means of edification in righteousness and truth and humanity. May we all leave this place with our good resolutions strengthened, our charities enlarged, and our hearts expanded in all embracing love toward our brethren of every tongue and clime. Bless, O Heavenly Father, the Order of which we are members, aid us in the good work of Benevolence and Charity, to which we are pledged, and give direction and success to our efforts Bless this edifice in the promotion of the good objects to which it has this day been set apart. Let Thy protecting care be over the brethren who here shall meet together; keep their feet upon the right path, and guide them by Thy power in the way everlasting; make them faithful to their duties, and zealous in every good word and work, so that when the solemn close of life comes, the soul of each may be stayed on Thee; and unto Thee, our God and Father, be ascribed glory and dominion and power, world without end. Amen.

**Grand Master.** — The brethren will now be seated.

*The following or other appropriate piece may be sung or omitted:*

THE SPREAD OF OUR ORDER.
Air — "*Missionary Hymn.*"

> Throughout this wide creation,
> O'er every land and sea,
> Odd Fellowship's extending
> Its deeds of Charity.
> With joy its steps attending,
> It guards the feet of youth
> From paths of sin and sorrow,

By Friendship, Love, and Truth.

Whene'er we meet together
For counsel or for aid,
May Love of purest virtue
Each brother's heart pervade,
With Temperance to guide us,
Assisted from above,
May all our acts be governed
By Friendship, Truth, and Love.

And bless, O God of Heaven
This lodge of brothers here;
O guard, protect, and shield them
From trouble, care, and fear!
Until Thou shalt transport them
To the Grand Lodge above,
To sing, with ransomed millions,
Of Friendship, Truth, and Love.

**Grand Master.** — My brethren, I trust that the solemn ceremonies of this occasion may not be lost upon our hearts. In setting apart this Hall for its noble purposes, we have renewed our vows to practice conscientiously the lessons of our beloved Order. Let us never forget the imperative command of our laws, "To visit the sick, to relieve the distressed, to bury the dead, and educate the orphan". Let us not forget, moreover, that besides these good works of charity, Odd Fellowship has high and important lessons to inculcate; lessons that, if attentively listened to, and practiced by all, would elevate the character of man, and hasten the coming of the promised day of universal peace and love. Brethren of _____ Lodge, we now again deliver into your hands [presenting the keys to the Noble Grand] this beautiful Temple you have elevated to our Order. Joy be within its walls and Peace a constant guest! May these walls never echo with the sound of an angry or unkind word. May all the influences that flow hence be good, and for good, now and forever. Amen.

*The choir will sing the following or other appropriate anthem, or omit, at the option of the officers:*

## SOUND THE GLAD CHORUS.
Air — "*Miriam's Song.*"


Sound the glad chorus! Let praises arise,
In works of our Order, to God in the skies.
Sound the glad chorus! Let praises arise,
In works of our Order, to God in the skies.
Sing! for the light of His Truth is advancing,
And darkness and suff'ring are fleeing away;
His Love, in its warmth, human souls is entrancing,
And Friendship, on earth, is asserting its sway.
Sound the glad chorus! Let praises arise,
in works of our Order, to God in the skies.
Sound the glad chorus! Let praises arise,
In works of our Order, to God in the skies.
To God in the skies, to God in the skies.

Welcome, Odd Fellowship! Praise to the Lord!

His Love is its buckler, His Truth is its sword.

Welcome, Odd Fellowship! Praise to the Lord!

His Love is its buckler His Truth is its sword.

Brethren raised up from despair are its story,

And orphans protected, its jewelry bright;

The tears of the widow—from gloom turned to glory,

Like the bow on a cloud—grow bright in its light.

Sound the glad chorus! Let praises ascend

To God, in the work of the heart and the hand.

Sound the glad chorus! Let praises ascend

To God, in the work of the heart and the hand,

The heart and the hand, the heart and the hand.

*The Grand Master or the Orator of the Day will now deliver an address appropriate to the occasion*

*The address or addresses being concluded—*

**Grand Master.** — The audience will please rise and unite in the

DOXOLOGY.
Tune — "*Old Hundred.*"

Praise God, from whom all blessings flow,

Praise Him, all creatures here below!

Praise Him above, ye heavenly host!

Praise Father, Son, and Holy Ghost.

**Grand Master.** — The Grand Chaplain will pronounce the benediction.

**Grand Chaplain.** — Now unto Him, who is able to keep you from falling, and to present you faultless before the presence of His glory with exceeding joy, I commend you and the whole family of man; and to Him, the only wise God, our Saviour, be glory and majesty, dominion and power, now and forever. Amen

# Dedication of a Corner-stone Ceremony

## CEREMONY OF LAYING THE CORNER-STONE
## OF AN ODD-FELLOWS' HALL
## 1904 (GENDER REVISED 2025)

*On the day appointed the Order shall assemble and each Body shall be opened in due form.  The procession shall then be formed in the order prescribed in Form 5.*

*If the hall is the property of a Grand or Subordinate lodge, the ceremony shall be performed by such Body, and the procession shall be under the control of its Marshal.  If the hall is the property of a Grand or Subordinate Encampment, the ceremony shall be performed by that Body, and the procession shall be under the control of its Marshal.  If the hall is joint property, that Body which shall receive the invitation to* lay the corner-stone, shall have charge, and the officiating officer shall be addressed by the title of the officer he or she represents, and the language of the ceremony shall be varied accordingly.

Should the ceremony be performed by the Sovereign Grand Master or his Deputy, the title of that officer should be substituted for Grand Master or Grand Patriarch, as the case may be.

An officer duly commissioned and officiating for a Grand Master or a Grand Patriarch, or as Noble Grand or Chief Patriarch shall be addressed by the title of the officer he or she represents.

If the ceremony is conducted by a Grand Lodge or a subordinate lodge, the Grand Secretary or Secretary, as the case may be, shall carry the documents, etc. for deposit in the box. The Grand Treasurer or Treasurer, as the case may be, shall carry the box to be deposited in the corner-stone.

The Grand Chaplain or Chaplain, as the case may be, shall carry the open Bible, on which is laid a wreath of flowers; the Grand Warden or Warden, as the case may be, shall carry a silver vessel containing water, and the Grand Conductor or Conductor, as the case may be, shall carry a silver vessel containing wheat. The Grand Master or Noble Grand, as the case may be, shall bear a gavel.

If the ceremony is conducted by a Grand Encampment or a Subordinate Encampment, the Grand Scribe or Scribe, as the case may be, shall carry the documents, etc., for deposit in the box, and the Grand Treasurer or Treasurer, as the case may be, shall carry the box to be deposited in the corner-stone.

*The Grand High Priest or High Priest, as the case may be, shall carry the open Bible, on which is laid a wreath of flowers; the Grand Senior Warden or Senior Warden, as the case may be, shall carry a silver vessel containing water; and the Grand Junior Warden or Junior Warden, as the case may be, shall carry a silver vessel containing wheat. The Grand Patriarch or Chief Patriarch, as the case may be, shall bear a crook.*

*Should the Sovereign Grand Master perform the ceremony, and the Sovereign Grand Lodge join in the procession, the Grand Marshal of that Body (with his or her aids) shall take position at the head of the column and have charge of the procession.*

*The Sovereign Grand Lodge will take position immediately after the Grand Bodies of the jurisdiction.*

*The Grand Secretary shall carry the documents, etc., for deposit in the box; the Grand Treasurer the box to be deposited in the corner-stone; the Grand Chaplain the open Bible, on which is laid a wreath of flowers; the Representative on his or her right a silver vessel containing water, and the Representative on his or her left a silver vessel containing wheat. The Sovereign Grand Master shall bear a gavel.*

*The procession, on reaching a convenient distance from the place of destination will halt and open to the right and left, so as to allow the principal officers to pass through; the remainder of the members, closing up in reversed order, will pass three times around the site of the building (if convenient), while the officiating officers take their places on a raised platform, erected contiguous to the northeast angle of the building; where the corner-stone is to be laid.*

**Grand Master.** — My brothers and sisters, we have assembled on this occasion to perform an interesting and important ceremony; one which we trust will have its proper influence upon your hearts and minds. The spot on which we stand has been selected upon which to erect a Temple to be consecrated to the great principles of our Order; and we are here today to inaugurate the enterprise by laying the first foundation or corner-stone in the structure, with the solemn ceremonies befitting such an occasion.

The work so auspiciously begun can be consummated only by persevering effort and patient industry; and we should enter upon it with a determination to carry it forward to completion, until its capstone shall be brought with rejoicings, and the edifice shall present beauty, symmetry, and proportion every way adapted to the uses and purposes for which it is designed.

Before proceeding to the immediate duties of the occasion, it is right and proper that we invoke the Divine blessing, without which no good work can succeed. Our Grand Chaplain will now address the Throne of Grace.

*The Grand Master gives three raps with the gavel.*

**Grand Chaplain.** — Thou who didst lay the foundations of the earth, and in whom alone we live and move and have our being, we beseech Thee of Thy great goodness to command Thy blessing to rest upon the work which we this day begin: honor it with Thine approving smile, and prosper it to its final accomplishment and to the glory of Thy great name, and the happiness of all mankind. Amen.

**Response by the members.** — So may it be.

*The Grand Secretary will then read the record to be deposited in the stone, with a list of the documents, coin, etc., and hand the list, with the articles to be deposited, to the Grand Treasurer, who will place the same in the box. The Grand Master, accompanied by the Grand Warden, Grand Chaplain, Grand Conductor, and Grand Treasurer, will then descend to the stone. The Grand Treasurer will then present the box to the Grand Master, who will place it in the cavity prepared for it, and adjust the lid. The stone will then be fitted accurately to its place.*

**Grand Master** *(receiving from the Grand Warden the vessel containing water).* — In the name of Friendship, as pure as this water *(sprinkling it three times upon the stone)*, I lay this corner-stone; and as it here forms the basis of this edifice, binding together in harmony and consistency the component parts of its superstructure, so may true Friendship ever constitute the foundation of our social fabric, and unite the family of man in one fraternal brotherhood.

**Response by the members.** — So may it be.

**Grand Master** *(receiving from the Grand Chaplain the wreath of flowers).* — In love, symbolized by these flowers *(strewing them three times over the stone)*, I lay this corner-stone; and as it underlies and supports this material temple, so may Love ever be the chief foundation - stone of the moral Temple of our Order; and the divine sentiment of Love ever animate the hearts of all its votaries.

**Response by the members.** — So may it be.

**Grand Master** *(receiving from the Grand Conductor the vessel containing wheat).* — In Truth, represented by this wheat *(strewing it three times over the stone)*, I lay this corner stone; trusting that Truth may ever prevail over error; and that its good seed, sown in our hearts, may bring forth its peaceful fruits in our lives. May the building here to be erected for the inculcation of Truth, ever remain unshaken by the storms of time; and our beloved Order ever rest securely upon the Rock of Ages.

**Response by the members.** — So may it be.

**Grand Master** *(giving three blows of the gavel upon the stone).* — In Benevolence and Charity, I lay this corner-stone, earnestly praying that as it is firmly fixed in this solid foundation, so may those cardinal virtues immutably repose in our organization, and be the constant practice of our Order.

**Response by the members.** — So may it be.

*The Architect will then deliver a trowel, with mortar, to the Grand Master, who shall spread it upon the corner-stone, and fix thereon a corresponding stone.*

**Grand Master.** — As this cement binds together the stones of the wall, so may the cement of brotherly affection bind us together during all the days of our lives here below; and so may the cement of Divine Love, in our Father's own good time, unite us as living stones in the Temple above, the "house not made with hands, eternal in the heavens."

**Response by the members.** — So may it be.

*The Grand Master and other officers will then return to the platform.*

**Grand Master.** — The Deputy Grand Master will now make the proper proclamation.

**Deputy Grand Master.** — By direction of the Grand Master, I declare this corner-stone duly laid according to regular and ancient form; and the building that is to rise upon it, devoted to the principles and work of Odd Fellowship.

**Grand Master.** — The Grand Chaplain will now address the Throne of Grace.

*The Grand Master gives three blows with the gavel.*

**Grand Chaplain.** — Almighty Architect of the Universe, who spake, and it was done; who commanded, and it stood fast; accept, we humbly pray Thee, the work of our hands this day performed, and strengthen us by Thy blessing to build upon this corner-stone a Temple in which shall be taught the great principles of Friendship, Love, and Truth, and where benevolence and Charity shall ever exercise their kindly offices, and be a safe refuge from the deluge of man's passions and the discordant elements of faction and selfishness.

Let Thy blessing abide with those who have zealously undertaken the work of building this edifice, and may they be enabled by Thy good Providence to carry it forward to entire completion. Bless, we pray Thee, those who are engaged in the construction of the building; preserve them by Thy mighty power from danger and accident while thus employed. Surround them with Thy protecting care, and may their health and lives be precious in Thy sight and keeping.

We earnestly invoke the continued smile of Thy approving countenance upon our widespread and beneficent Order. Give to it, we beseech Thee, the guidance of Thy Holy Spirit, and prosper it in the thing whereunto Thou hast ordained it. Give it success in all its aims and efforts to benefit mankind. May it ever build upon the sure foundations of Truth and Righteousness; and ever exert a moral influence over the minds and consciences of its entire membership.

Command Thy rich blessing upon the poor, the needy, the friendless, and the destitute, and open up the way and the means for their relief. Bless the widow and the orphan in their affliction, and give unto us sympathizing hearts and open hands to aid them and provide for their wants.

And we pray Thee, God of Love, that the period may soon come when discord and strife and war shall cease from the face of the earth, and the reign of peace shall be universally established - when the law of Love shall control all hearts; and the nations, tribes, and kindreds of the earth shall be united together as a band of brothers, and shall acknowledge Thee as their Father; and to Thee we will ascribe all majesty, power, and dominion now and forever. Amen.

**Grand Master.** — Brothers and Sisters, the duty assigned us has been performed. We have begun a good work, which it remains for you to finish. Having entered upon so important an enterprise, fail not to carry it forward to success, which I am confident you will achieve. I trust you will here erect a Temple worthy of being dedicated to the great cause of Humanity, and which will reflect honor upon your zeal in its behalf.

*The Grand Master gives three blows with the gavel.*

**Grand Chaplain** (This may be pronounced AFTER the oration, if desired). — The Lord bless you and keep you; the Lord make his face to shine upon you and be gracious unto you; the Lord lift up his fatherly countenance upon you, and give you peace. Amen.

*Oration.*

*The procession will then reform in the same order and return to the place of starting.*

# WEDDING CEREMONY (UNOFFICIAL)

## ODD FELLOWS WEDDING CEREMONY (UNOFFICIAL)
### BY REV. LINNEA BREDENBERG
### PAST GRAND CHAPLAIN

*The lodge room or function hall is arranged as normal with the possible addition of extra seating to accommodate all the guests. An altar is set up in the center of the room. Open space is left in front of the dais with the Noble Grand's station to allow for escort and introduction of dignitaries. A Holy Bible or alternatively a large stone is placed on the Secretary's desk or a similarly located table. A vessel of water, basket of flower petals, and basket of wheat are placed on the Treasurer's desk or a similarly located table.*

*The Noble Grand and Lodge Chaplain or Clergy Member stand in the front of the room facing the audience. The Chaplain should have the rings in their possession. The Water Bearer, Flower Bearer, and Wheat Bearer are seated in the audience. The other Lodge Officers are seated at their regular stations. Dignitaries, including family and friends whom the couple wishes to honor, form a line outside the lodge, followed by the couple to be married.*

## Processional

*The Warden and Conductor lead the procession in. Once they reach the center of the floor, the Dignitaries directly behind them peel off to each side, leading their portion of procession into a line facing the front. The couple enters the line in the center of the floor in front of the Noble Grand's station.*

**Noble Grand.** — Warden and Conductor, you will escort the Dignitaries to their seats.

*The Warden and Conductor escort the Dignitaries to seats.*

**Noble Grand.** — The audience will please rise and be attentive while the Chaplain offers prayer.

**Chaplain.** — O God, our creator and preserver, who didst lay the foundations of the Earth, and in whom alone we live and move and have our being, we beseech Thee of Thy great goodness to command Thy blessing to rest upon the work which we, this day, begin: honor in it with Thine approving smile, prosper it to its final accomplishment and to the glory of Thy great name. Grant happiness to this loving couple who are today to be joined together in marriage, that their union shall enrich the lives of the both, that together, they may work in harmony with their community toward the greater benefaction of humankind. Amen.

**All.** — So may it be.

**Noble Grand.** — The audience may be seated.

## Introductions

**Bride or Groom.** — Friends, Family, Brothers and Sisters in Odd Fellowship, we have invited you here today to witness the joining of two Odd Fellows in the covenant of matrimony.

**Bride or Groom.** — We gather here to sanctify the beginning of our new life together, our journey to build a household founded on those same principles which brought us together, and to help us bless and lay the cornerstone of our life together.

**Bride or Groom.** — At this time we invite all elective and past elective officers of all grand bodies to rise and introduce yourselves.

*All elective and past elective officers rise. One at a time, they state their name and current or highest title only and are then seated.*

**Bride or Groom.** — We invite all family members and honored guests of the Bride and Groom to rise and introduce yourselves.

*All family members and honored guests to be introduced rise. One at a time, they state their name and relationship to the couple and are then seated.*

*[Optional: The Noble Grand or Chaplain may also read the names of departed lodge members and family using the following charge so that they may be present in spirit: We also honor the memory of <read the list*

*of names> who have departed the world but are still present with us in spirit.]*

## Purification Prior to Vows

*The Warden retrieves the large stone or Holy Bible from the Secretary's station and presents it to the Chaplain. The Chaplain steps forward to stand between the Bride and Groom.*

**Chaplain.** — The work of Odd Fellowship has many purposes, chief among them, to build a lodge for its members that, together, they may hail it as a second home. In uniting themselves as a family, <Groom's Name> and <Bride's Name>, in both Odd Fellowship and in life, have chosen to begin the sacred endeavor of building, together, that first home: a place of domestic tranquility, a temple devoted to a unique friendship and love, and a shared truth. From the foundation of marriage, husband and wife, having learned the lessons that we all hail as the best defense against the ills of life, commit their lives to one another, to the benefit of both. Though there is much work yet to be done, today we lay the cornerstone.

*The Chaplain lays the Holy Bible or large stone upon the altar. If the Bible is used, the Bride and Groom are to be purified below, but if the stone is used, the stone is purified to represent the couple's home.*

**Chaplain.** — You will now join me at this altar representing your future home.

*The couple steps forward to stand at the altar.*

*The Water Bearer rises and stands before the couple. The Conductor retrieves the vessel of water from the Treasurer's station and presents it to the Water Bearer.*

**Water Bearer.** — In Friendship, as pure as this water *(sprinkling the couple or stone three times)*, I bless and consecrate this union, that deep friendship may ever serve as the wellspring of their relationship.

*The Flower Bearer rises and stands before the couple. The Conductor retrieves the basket of flowers from the Treasurer's station and presents it to the Flower Bearer.*

**Flower Bearer.** — In Love, symbolized by these flowers *(throwing petals over the couple or stone three times)*, I bless and consecrate this union, that Love may ever be the foundation stone of their home together.

*The Wheat Bearer rises and stands before the couple. The Conductor retrieves the basket of wheat from the Treasurer's station and presents it to the Wheat Bearer.*

**Wheat Bearer.** — In Truth, represented by this wheat *(strewing the wheat over over the couple or stone three times)*, I bless and consecrate this union, that among them Truth shall ever prevail over error, and that it's good seed, sown in their hearts, may bring forth the bounty of peace. May they rest securely on the Rock of Ages in Truth, unshaken by the storms of change and time.

## Vows

**Chaplain.** — I ask you both now to come forward and lay your hands upon this, the cornerstone of your life together.

*The couple steps forward to stand before the altar and lays their hands atop the Holy Bible or large stone.*

*The vows below are provided as examples. These or any vows of the couple's choosing may be used:*

## Example One

**Chaplain.** — Do you, <Groom's Name>, take <Bride's Name>, in the spirit of Friendship, Love, and Truth, to be your lawful wife? Do you promise ever to place your faith in her and her word as an Odd Fellow? Do you promise to love her, and to share with her all that is yours? Do you promise to work together with her, to hold her close to you in all matters, as your dearest friend?

**Groom.** — I do.

**Chaplain.** — Do you, <Bride's Name>, take <Groom's Name>, in the spirit of Friendship, Love, and Truth, to be your lawful husband? Do you promise ever to place your faith in him and his word as an Odd fellow? Do you promise to love him, and to share with him all that is yours? Do you promise to work together with him, to hold him close to you in all matters, as your dearest friend?

**Bride.** — I do.

## Example Two

**Chaplain.** — <Groom's Name>, please read your vows to <Bride's Name>.

**Groom.** — I, <Groom's Name>, take you, <Bride's Name>, as my friend, partner, and wife, in the spirit of Friendship, Love, and Truth. I promise to put my faith in you, in your honesty as an Odd Fellow, and in your word as your bond. I promise to love and protect you, so long as we both shall live, and to share with you all that is mine. I take you as my helpmate, and I promise to work together with you in all matters, regarding you for forevermore as my dearest friend.

**Chaplain.** — <Bride's Name>, please read your vows to <Groom's Name>.

**Bride.** — I, <Bride's Name>, take you, <Groom's Name>, as my friend, partner, and husband, in the spirit of Friendship, Love, and Truth. I promise to put my faith in you, in your honesty as an Odd Fellow, and in your word as your bond. I promise to love and protect you, so long as we both shall live, and to share with you all that is mine. I take you as my helpmate, and I promise to work together with you in all matters, regarding you for forevermore as my dearest friend.

## Exchange of Rings

**Chaplain.** — So be it. Let the rings be passed to the front of the room, through the hands of the people assembled to add their warmth and good wishes to the union.

*The Warden retrieves the rings from the Chaplain and carries them to the rear of the room. The Warden hands them to a guest in the back and oversees the process of rings being passed through the hands of the family, friends, and members assembled. Once the rings have been passed through the entire audience, the Warden collects them and delivers them to the bride and groom.*

**Chaplain.** — <Groom's Name>, as you place this ring on <Bride's Name>'s finger, please repeat after me: "With this ring, I thee wed."

*The Groom repeats the phrase and places the ring on the Bride's finger.*

**Chaplain.** — <Bride's Name>, as you place this ring on <Groom's Name>'s finger, please repeat after me: "With this ring, I thee wed."

*The Bride repeats the phrase and places the ring on the Groom's finger.*

## Blessing the Union

*The people chosen to give blessings advance one at a time to stand before the couple. The blessings below are provided as examples. These or any blessings of the couple's choosing may be used:*

**An Odd Fellow or Rebekah.** — May your hearts ever be bound together by the golden chain of Friendship.

**An Odd Fellow or Rebekah.** — May you each give and receive Love in abundance.

**An Odd Fellow or Rebekah.** — May you ever speak the Truth to one another.

**Patriarch or Matriarch.** — May your Faith never depart you

**Patriarch or Matriarch.** — May your Hope shine brightly, even in the darkest times.

**Patriarch or Matriarch.** — May you ever be generous in Charity.

**Chevalier or Lady.** — May all of your works strengthen the cause of Universal Justice

## Concluding Charge

**Past Grand.** — My Brother and Sister, the vows you have taken are to one another, but also of a purpose with greater meaning than you may at first realize. Through the sharing of all that is yours with one another, you have created a stable platform, from which you may better serve your lodge, your community, and all who are in need. It is a place of refuge, a place of reflection, and a place of hospitality. Upon it, may you both prosper through long and fruitful lives.

**Chaplain.** — I now pronounce you husband and wife.

## Presentation and Recessional

*The Warden and Conductor escort the Bride, Groom, and Chaplain to the center of the floor.*

**Chaplain.** — It is my pleasure and privilege to introduce <Groom's Name> and <Bride's Name>, who are duly married and are joined in Friendship, Love, and Truth, in their hearts and in the eyes of our Creator and Preserver. Let us celebrate them in the spirit of Odd Fellowship.

*The Warden and Conductor escort the honorees and family to stand before the couple, then escort them out, the Bride and Groom falling into line behind them, during which time an ode may be sung.*

# On Virtues

## Friendship

Friendship is the first of the three main virtues of Odd Fellowship. It is the glue that binds those who would otherwise be strangers into chosen Brothers and Sisters. In a world that feels more disconnected despite all the modes of communication available, knowing one has friends at lodge can be the difference between hope and despair.

*1 Samuel 20:42: Jonathan said to David, "Go in peace, for we have sworn friendship with each other in the name of the LORD, saying, 'The LORD is witness between you and me, and between your descendants and my descendants forever.' " Then David left, and Jonathan went back to the town.*

A lot happens in the story of Jonathan and David. Yet in all the action, our Odd Fellow take on their relationship culminates in the oath they take with each other. The phrase that ends that passage is unspoken in our exemplification of that Covenant of Friendship: "Then David left, and Jonathan went back to the town." That's the real test of friendship isn't it? The moment ends and we go our separate ways, but unlike a random stranger with whom we may make small talk or assist along our way and then never seen again, our friends stay in our thoughts and our hearts.

When our bodies are hungry, we go into the kitchen, pull open the refrigerator, and look for something to eat. When our hearts are hungry, we seek out a friend to nourish them. We know that they are there when we need them, so we don't need to fear starving for connection.

Sometimes, though, when a person needs connection, they are least able to reach out for it. There are many reasons why a member may feel unable to reach out; depression, embarrassment, and fear rank high among those. It is up to you to be the friend you swore to be and to seek out a member who hasn't been around. Find out how they are doing and connect with them on their terms. Remember it is a Covenant of Friendship, not a Contract of Friendship; you owe your end even if the other party has not met expectations.

As the saying goes, 'A friend in need is a friend indeed.' Let us make a slight Odd Fellow-focused change to it, though: 'A friend in need is a friend in deed.' Empathy and sympathy are valuable, but action is of greater value. When a member is in need, be a friend in deed.[1]

---

1. *I.O.O.F. News*, Vol. 27, Issue 5, Sovereign Grand Lodge (2024)

## Love & Charity

The Degree of Brotherly Love beautifully reminds us that everyone has a claim upon our care and compassion. In our degree and in the parable upon which it is based, only slight attention is paid to those who did not help.

*LUKE 10:31-32 — A priest happened to be going down the same road, and when he saw the man, he passed by on the other side. So too, a Levite, when he came to the place and saw him, passed by on the other side.*

It is worth taking a second look at these passages and reconsidering them in light of the purpose of the Odd Fellows. We put a lot of effort into various charitable programs that help those who are not our members, and that is in keeping with the overarching theme of showing Brotherly Love and Charity. But we also need to ask ourselves if we are being like the priest and Levite regarding aiding our own. After all, the Odd Fellowship was created to be a mutual benefit society.

I am sure the priest and the Levite would have had reasonable justifications for why they could not stop and help the suffering traveler. They likely had vital work to do, carrying out the responsibilities of their offices, and I am sure they would have congratulated themselves on all the good works they did through their duties. What is the suffering of one of their own when weighed against all the other important works that they did?

It is everything. That is especially so in the Odd Fellows. Why join if you can reap all the benefits while not being a member? Why join if you have to take on all the burden and cost of helping others when your needs go unmet? The days of paying out regular benefits to members for sickness, job loss, etc., may be all but gone, but there are still ways for the suffering members to get help from those of their lodge without having to rely on the kindness of a stranger.

Look after your own members who may be struggling and do not pass them by on the other side while on your way to do something else for the good of the Order. The good of the Order is tending to the needs of the members first, so that they can then contribute to our efforts. Ask yourself what you and your lodge can do to help your own members. Pass the hat for your own member relief fund before passing it for other things. Not instead of other things, just before them.

It is a wonderful thing to help the suffering stranger on the roadside, just remember not to pass by our own in need while going to help others.[2]

## Truth

What is Truth? There are times when it seems that truth has become entirely subjective. We talk about "your truth" and "my truth". Is that Truth? I've always considered these "truths" to be personal experiences and perceptions of truth rather than different truths. Somewhere along the line, our judgments of right and wrong have become the arbiters of truth. We feel that the truth of a thing is dependent upon our judgment of its rightness. We will argue that everyone is entitled to their own opinions, but not to their own facts, while simultaneously claiming that each person can have their own truth; a dichotomy of thought that inherently divides facts from truth. It has become increasingly difficult for people to come together on common ground.

---

2. *I.O.O.F. News*, Vol. 27, Issue 6, Sovereign Grand Lodge (2024)

These social difficulties follow us everywhere we go, including into our lodges. We refrain from discussions of politics and religious topics in our meetings, but the baggage we bring into our lodges of not just disagreeing with others but that the disagreements we have are fundamental and that our view is our truth and therefore the other side must not only have a different viewpoint or experience but also be inherently wrong. It is hard to leave disputes and strife to others and move in harmony when we feel we're not living in the same reality.

The Third Degree is the Degree of Truth. It is where we, as Odd Fellows, should look first to resolve these feelings and find our common ground – the truth upon which our Order is based. One of the symbols of the Degree of Truth is the Holy Bible. It is so because it is the source of our lessons. One does not need to be of a Judeo-Christian faith to understand the lessons we pull from the Bible, but there is a need to accept that they are fundamentally true. If they are not, then the teachings of Odd Fellowship are built upon a foundation of sand.

*Psalm 119:160: The entirety of Your word is truth, And every one of Your righteous judgments endures forever.*

Is the lesson of the Friendship between Jonathan and David not true? Is the lesson of Love in the parable of the Good Samaritan not true? Is the lesson of Divine Truth not true? Is the existence of a Supreme Being not true?

Believing that all those things are true is the fundamental common ground from which we build our Order. They are the truths upon which all Odd Fellows agree, without which we are not united as one band. We would be separate sticks if each member had their "own truth" of what Friendship, Love, and Truth mean. We are united as one through the simple acceptance that there is Truth in the world and that we act together upon these three main truths as expressed in the Bible. We each have our own experiences and perceptions, our own religious beliefs and practices, but we are united in the simple Truth that we believe in a Supreme Being.[3]

## Hope & Faith

The Encampment teaches us that Faith, Hope, and Charity are the columns of support for Friendship, Love, and Truth. Previously, we have discussed charity in the context of brotherly love, and the example of the Good Samaritan contrasted with the priest and Levite. We have also discussed faith in the context of divine truth. But we have not touched on Hope.

The Golden Rule Degree is not focused on Hope but rather serves to expand the lesson from the Second Degree of Brotherly Love. Where do we then turn as Odd Fellows to understand the role of Hope in our Order?

I turn to our Odd Fellows Funeral Service. It is where I feel the importance and beauty of hope is most powerfully illustrated: "How cheerless the home of the dead when unrelieved by the prospect of immortal life! But hope remains over man's last resting place like an arch bright with life everlasting, which, based upon earth, extends far into the sacred realms of eternity." It is no accident that the next line in the ritual equates that hope with faith. The two are inextricably linked. One cannot have hope without faith. You have to believe in a possibility, have faith in that possibility, for you to sustain hope for that possibility. You lose hope

---

3. *I.O.O.F. News*, Vol. 28, Issue 1, Sovereign Grand Lodge (2025)

when you lose faith in yourself, your community, or God. But the reverse can also be true.

People are frequently hopeful. We look forward to things. We buy a raffle ticket. We plan a vacation. In a million ways, we live lives of hope. Even when we suffer anxiety, it could be viewed as the outcome of our inner conflict between our hopes and our fears. Or when we suffer depression, it could be viewed as the result of our hopes being dashed. In so many ways, hope is a constant beacon in our lives. Just pause for a moment and think about all the little hopes you have in a day, from hoping there isn't too much traffic, hoping your back will hurt less, or hoping there's still enough milk left for your coffee since you forgot to get more.

Now, I ask you to realize that if you have hope, you have faith. Sometimes life can become tough and very bleak. A person can feel like they've lost faith. They can feel lost. That feeling is a form of blindness. But if, when feeling like that, one can realize that there are still small hopes in so many ways, even if the only hope is to feel better, that is also evidence of faith. You cannot hope for what you do not believe is possible and belief in the possible is a form of faith.

For me, it's not just a form of faith. It is faith. As we are told in *Matthew 19:26: Jesus looked at them and said, "With man this is impossible, but with God all things are possible."*

Even when it feels like the world is falling apart, like tragedy and cruelty infest the world, or like the weight of loss is crushing, and some may feel a crisis of faith, I say to pause and see your hope, because hope is faith in a different form. If you have hope, your faith is not gone. Likewise, if you have faith, you will always have hope.

Our funeral ritual may speak of death and hope of immortality, but the lesson applies equally to life. Hope relieves our discomfort and shines as a practical symbol of faith. It is like the rainbow, which forms as light passes through the moisture in the sky. The rainbow is hope: the beautiful arch that connects you with the light of faith through your stormy troubles. And I am thankful for it.[4]

## Fidelity

Fidelity is more than a mere promise or obligation; the steadfast commitment holds our Order together through calm and storm. In the context of Odd Fellowship, Fidelity calls us to stand firm by one another, to honor our guiding principles of Friendship, Love, and Truth, and to remain unwavering even when tested by adversity. It is not simply the act of being present; it is the profound choice to be loyal in word and deed, offering steadfast support as we uphold the unity of our fellowship.

When we speak of Fidelity, we speak of a type of loyalty that secures and enriches our communal bonds. It begins by binding us to something larger than ourselves: our shared ideals and our collective purpose. Fidelity is first demonstrated in the unspoken assurance that each member is prepared to walk alongside another, whether in times of trouble, uncertainty, or celebration. This spirit of commitment is what allows Odd Fellows to function as one family. We pledge to remain loyal to the Order's tenets and the individuals who comprise our community, giving and receiving support as needs arise.

---

4. *I.O.O.F. News,* Vol. 28, Issue 2, Sovereign Grand Lodge (2025)

It is fitting that Fidelity is the special virtue of the Rebekah branch. We find the most powerful illustration of Fidelity in the Old Testament story of Ruth and Naomi. Even though Ruth faced an uncertain future, she committed herself to her mother-in-law with these words:

*Ruth 1:16: Where you go I will go, and where you stay I will stay. Your people will be my people, and your God will be my God.*

This passage reveals Fidelity at its most courageous: a willingness to step into unknown territory for the sake of another, guided by love and devotion rather than self-interest. In Odd Fellowship, we, too, are called to demonstrate this kind of faithfulness: to stand beside our members, to share in their burdens, and to offer steadfast support regardless of the circumstances.

Through Fidelity, we ensure that our shared values continue to flourish, both within our halls and in the communities we serve. We do this by extending helping hands, keeping our promises, and speaking truthfully even when it is difficult. Genuine Fidelity does not demand perfection, but it does require sincerity and perseverance. When we commit to an ideal or to a brother or sister in the Order, we affirm that the relationship is worth our time, effort, and sacrifice.

Fidelity weaves itself through every dimension of Odd Fellowship: it sustains our friendships, shapes our demonstrations of love, and keeps us anchored to truth. In a world where promises can be fleeting and loyalties uncertain, Fidelity stands as a steady compass, guiding us back to our highest values and reminding us of our duty to each other. By striving to live this virtue daily, we renew the bonds of our brotherhood and embody the enduring spirit of Odd Fellowship.[5]

## Universal Justice

The Patriarchs Militant is not just a group of men and women in fancy uniforms and shiny swords. The branch aspires to promote, and carries its swords to defend, the most needed principle in human society: Universal Justice.

Justice, in its highest form, transcends any single individual or group. It involves recognizing the inherent worth and dignity of every person, ensuring that fairness guides our actions rather than favoritism or prejudice. Within the framework of Odd Fellowship, Universal Justice functions as a cornerstone, reminding us that our commitment to Friendship, Love, and Truth must be applied equally to all people regardless of their background, station, or creed.

From its earliest beginnings, Odd Fellowship has urged its members to practice a kind of Justice that reaches beyond mere legal definitions, focusing instead on moral and ethical fairness rooted in compassion and respect. This sense of Justice compels us to look not only at our own inner circles but also at the broader world around us. Each time we undertake charitable initiatives, welcome new faces into our halls, or advocate for the well-being of our local communities, we actively pursue a vision of Universal Justice. We affirm that every individual's rights and dignity deserve safeguarding, and we uphold the principle that we must do right

---

by others simply because it is just, not merely because it is expedient or expected.

In the Old Testament, the prophet Micah poses a challenge that resonates deeply with our pursuit of Universal Justice:

*Micah 6:8: He has shown you, O mortal, what is good. And what does the LORD require of you? To act justly and to love mercy and to walk humbly with your God.*

This scripture places Justice on equal footing with mercy and humility. Acting justly means more than enforcing rules; it is about nurturing fairness in our relationships and broader social structures, ensuring no one is overlooked or devalued. For Odd Fellows, this charge is not limited to our lodge rooms; it extends into our homes, workplaces, and the global community, reflecting a sincere desire to see equitable treatment for all.

Yet practicing Universal Justice is rarely straightforward. It demands self-awareness, a willingness to examine our own actions and biases, to recognize when our judgments might be tainted by selfishness or prejudice, and to correct course accordingly. It also demands empathy. If we are to treat everyone justly, we must strive to understand their experiences, struggles, and needs, refusing to let differences become excuses for dismissal or discrimination. In doing so, we bring our principles of Friendship and Love to life, tempering Justice with compassion and forging bonds that transcend divisions of age, race, culture, or belief.

Moreover, Universal Justice requires that we embrace Truth as a guide. When we respond to real-world issues, we must be committed to honest assessment and transparent conversation. Only by confronting facts openly and without fear can we take steps toward truly impartial justice.

In standing up for what is right, especially when it is inconvenient or uncomfortable, we honor the Odd Fellows' legacy of moral courage.

Ultimately, Universal Justice in Odd Fellowship is both a promise and a process. It is a promise that our doors and hearts remain open to all who seek friendship and support. It is a process requiring active engagement, a continual dedication to making fair, compassionate choices in our everyday lives. As we strive to "act justly" and "walk humbly," we embody our Order's noblest ideals, extending the reach of Friendship, Love, and Truth beyond ourselves and into every interaction. In doing so, we uphold a key tenet of Odd Fellowship: that lasting fraternity must be built on a just foundation, one that seeks the betterment of all humanity.[6]

---

6. *I.O.O.F. News*, Vol. 28, Issue 4, Sovereign Grand Lodge (2025)

# REGALIA

Each branch has unique regalia for the office of Chaplain, although they are all similar, except for the High Priest of the Encampment.

## Odd Fellows

A jewel of silver or white metal with an ornamental frame and the emblem of an open Bible attached on the front, and the other side plain, suspended from a white or silver collar.  Item #1317D - Chaplain[1]

## Rebekahs

A jewel of silver or white metal with an ornamental frame and the emblem of an open Bible attached on the front above the word "Chaplain", and the other side plain, suspended from a pink and green collar.  Item #2237[2]

---

1. *Odd Fellow Lodge Regalia,* Sovereign Grand Lodge (2024) p. 1

2. *Rebekah Lodge Regalia,* Sovereign Grand Lodge (2024) p. 1

## Encampment

A jewel of gold or yellow metal with an ornamental frame in a triangular shape, and with the design of an open Bible attached on the front, and the other side plain, suspended from a purple collar.  Item #3158 – High Priest[3]

## Canton

A circular sleeve patch with a red background bordered in silver with an open Bible in the center thereof.  Item #51504

---

3. *Encampment Regalia*, Sovereign Grand Lodge (2024) p. 1

4. *Uniform Regulations for the Patriarchs Militant Army, Sovereign Grand Lodge* (2024) p. 42